Landscape

architecture

First published in the United States of America by
Rockport Publishers, Inc.
33 Commercial Street
Gloucester, Massachusetts 01930-5089
Telephone: (508) 282-9590
Fax: (508) 283-2742

Distributed to the book trade and art trade in the
United States by
North Light Books, an imprint of
F & W Publications
1507 Dana Avenue
Cincinnati, Ohio 45207
Telephone: (800) 289-0963

Other Distribution by
Rockport Publishers, Inc.
Gloucester, Massachusetts 01930-5089

ISBN 1-56496-101-X

10 9 8 7 6 5 4 3 2 1

Manufactured in China

Design: PandaMonium Designs, Boston

page 78: The Greensward Plan of Central Park, ca. 1857, courtesy
of New York City Parks & Recreation Photo Archive.
Photo by Bob Laurence.
page 148: "Boys in a Pasture," 1874, Winslow Homer. The Hayden Collection.
Courtesy, Museum of Fine Arts, Boston, Massachusetts.

Cover photo: Hotel, theme restaurant, and bungalows at Mauna Lani Resort,
South Kohala, Hawaii, USA, Belt Collins. Photo by Bill Schildge.

Back cover photos: (top) Gainey Ranch Golf Club, Scottsdale, Arizona, USA
JMP Golf Design Group. Photo by Joann Dost.
(bottom) Appalachian Regional Educational Center, Berea,
Kentucky, USA, John Tillman Lyle, FASLA.

Landscape
architecture

Steven Moorhead
Editor

Gordon Grice
Coordinating Editor

ROCKPORT
PUBLISHERS

Rockport Publishers
Gloucester, Massachusetts

ACKNOWLEDGMENTS

We wish to acknowledge J. William Thompson, M.A., MLA, ASLA, Senior Editor of *Landscape Architecture* magazine, and E. Lynn Miller, MLA, FASLA, Emeritus Professor of Landscape Architecture at Pennsylvania State University, for their generous assistance in the selection of contributors.

We would also like to thank Forrec President Jeff McNair and Executive Vice Presidents Gordon Dorrett and Steve Rhys for their help and support; project coordinator, Arthur Furst; and at Rockport Publishers, editor Martha Wetherill and designer Heather Yale.

CONTENTS

INTRODUCTION

Landscape architecture: a profession only a little over a century old; an art as old as human existence.

—Norman T. Newton,
Design on the Land, 1971

The art of landscape architecture predates the profession by thousands of years. Ancient cultures venerated the garden as one of the highest achievements of a civilized society. Descriptions of the magnificent gardens of ancient Babylon and Egypt have survived, even though the landmarks themselves have not. Subsequent Greek and Roman civilizations contributed the arts of urban design and space planning. But it was not until the last half of the nineteenth century that the title *landscape architect* was officially used to describe a practitioner of landscape design. Invented by Calvert Vaux and Frederick Law Olmsted, it was intended to suggest an approach to a landscape that, as Norman Newton writes, would reflect "the same relation that an architect bears toward a building with the essential emphasis on *design*."

Despite its well-documented history, landscape architecture isn't an easy profession to define. Even members of the profession have difficulty rendering a description that captures all of its nuances and possibilities. Today there are many more concerns relating to the landscape and built environment than ever existed in the past: disappearing habitats and environmental degradation on a global scale, overcrowding in urban areas, a loss of privacy due to population density and the intrusion of commercial enterprise in every aspect of life, blurring and changing cultural identities and demographic balances, and the apparent triumph of profit over public benefit, to name a few. The abundance of ideas about how to deal with these concerns makes the possibility of a simple description of landscape architecture more remote every day.

This book offers a broad definition of landscape architecture by example, presenting the current work of thirty-one offices and individuals. Some writers have suggested that landscape architecture cannot be defined

as simply what landscape architects do—a lazy explanation, they say, that does little more than beg the question. We disagree, and have taken the position that there is, in fact, no better way to define it. Rather than trying to decide beforehand what constitutes landscape architecture and then selecting work that reflects this preconceived ideal, we have instead selected offices whose work is exciting, challenging, and current. We present this work as our broad definition of landscape architecture in its many configurations at the end of the twentieth century.

Landscape architecture constitutes an approach to solving problems—a method as well as a product. In the course of their training, landscape architects acquire a variety of skills that may be applied to many kinds of problems. In this book, we present the work on an office-by-office rather than a project-by-project basis, so that a method of approach is more apparent. Also, while some of the offices presented here dwell in specific areas of the profession (such as public spaces, private gardens, or restorations), others are more general. Accordingly, we have not tried to classify the offices or the work by project type. This gives the advantage of viewing a landscape solution in more than one way. The restoration of a natural habitat may also serve as a public park; a public park may also be an entertainment facility. The resulting product may defy categorization entirely.

We include in this broad category examples of work by landscape architects that has rarely, if ever, appeared in books on the subject: golf course design, leisure and entertainment design, indoor landscaping, and the work of public agencies. The rarity of this work in print is in contrast to its increasing importance in our built environment. Golf courses, for example, represent an idealized version of landscape, and are becoming more and more important in the Middle and Far East. Leisure and entertainment design has become a powerful force in international development, and its best examples employ the talent of many landscape architects. Indoor landscaping has become increasingly important as a result of our modern technical ability to create fully climate-controlled, unobstructed spaces that are large enough to accommodate artificial lakes, rivers, and mountains. Public agencies such as the City of New York Department of Parks and Recreation, and the City and County of San

Some of the work shown on these pages may fit neatly into everyone's idea of normal professional activity. Other examples are far from the norm. In trying to achieve as broad a definition of the profession as possible, we have included an equally broad range of offices, from local to international, from theoretical to practical, from sole practitioners to multi-office corporations. All of our contributors are landscape architects and consider themselves to be practicing landscape architecture in a significant way, and in every case, we think so too.

One area of the profession that is frequently overlooked and under-represented is what might be called "everyday" landscape architecture; not the kind you have to dress up for, or read an article about in order to understand. If some books on the subject of landscape architecture err in the direction of too much theory, we hope to compensate by erring perhaps on the side of too much practicality.

Francisco Department of Public Works perform miracles of accessible landscape architecture, but have no marketing budget, so if you don't visit their handiwork, you may never know of it.

This brings us back to Frederick Law Olmsted and the origins of our profession. Central Park is today one of the many parks under the care of the New York Department of Parks and Recreation, but it was on that project, in 1863, that *landscape architect* became an honest designation. In the years since, much has changed in the demands placed on the design of an urban park, and on the demands of landscape architecture in general, but the ideal remains the same: to create environments of quality and delight. In the pages of this book, you will find examples of many forms that may help you to understand and appreciate this ancient art and recent profession.

Steven Moorhead, FCSLA, ASLA

J. Robert Anderson, ASLA

The work of J. Robert Anderson embraces a broad palette of planning and design, including site preservation, water conservation, and the selection of native plants and regional materials that respond to the rugged Texas Hill Country. His firm gracefully integrates large architectural projects into difficult, environmentally sensitive habitats.

Central Texas' geology, endangered species, threatened aquifers, and dwindling tree cover are given primary consideration. The firm's respect for the state's history, culture, and countryside is reflected in landscape designs that require little water and are characterized by natural plantings and features. As Texas' growing urban areas are filled with gardens, plantings, and forms that are foreign to the state, the creative work of this firm proudly borrows influence, inspiration, and integrity from a rough, rugged landscape.

Robert Anderson's award-winning firm has championed the use of native plants for a

decade and continues to test them in a diverse set of micro-niches and project types. Natural formations of stone have been used by the firm to shape ponds, pools, walks, planting beds, walls, and arbors. Compositions created by hand-hewn rock terraces and billowy native grasses are especially prominent in his work.

In addition to residential projects, the marriage of architecture and Texas landscape is seen in J. Robert Anderson's projects for universities, schools, memorials, and cemeteries. Although less akin to natural shapes and forms, this work is designed to blend in an architectural sense.

The firm's orientation always has been toward design connecting with the surroundings rather than dominating. "We've been altering and changing the face of the earth too long," Anderson says. "We need to give something back in the image of our Creator."

National Wildflower Research Center
Austin, TX, USA

The Wildflower Research Center is a botanical garden for native plants comprising ten buildings, five major open space units, twenty-three theme gardens, water features, and rainwater harvesting.

▲
The central plaza of flagstone is surrounded by stone buildings. Here, native plants are arranged by their water needs in formal beds.

◄ At the entrance walk approaching the complex, a stone cistern catches rainwater and stores it for drip irrigation of native plants.

Pickerel weed, arrowhead, and sedges punctuate the edges of the water garden. Stone shapes suggest the historic influence of Spanish Mission construction.

Twenty-three demonstration gardens are used for display and research of native plants, including endangered species, tall grasses, and studies on pollination.

This garden retreat was designed for fall color with masses of Maximillian sunflowers, a favorite of Lady Bird Johnson, founder of the National Wildflower Research Center.

The pool in the central plaza often is mistaken for a natural spring. Stonework creating the spring was recycled from the site.

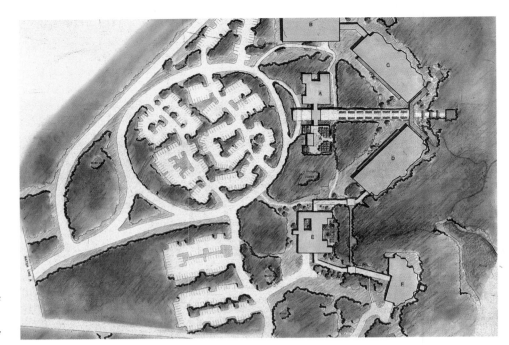

Schlumberger Well Services, Austin Systems Center
Austin, TX, USA

At this computer engineering campus, landscape planning called for site preservation first, design second to integrate large buildings into the Hill Country setting while following the ridge line of the canyon.

◄ The natural forms of the Schlumberger site are transformed at night through careful placement of concealed lighting.

▲
A pergola entwined with wisteria connects the
entrance building with the core of the campus.

▲
Winding through the fall wildflowers, this path
descends from parking areas to the workplace.

▲
Contrasting with surrounding woodlands, this
courtyard contains a grid of pear trees in gravel,
reflecting the company's French history and culture while repeating the colors of the building.

Pflugerville John Connally High School
Austin, TX, USA

Clump grasses such as Big Muhly are tough survivors needing little maintenance from a growing school system. Bunchgrass and stone befit the Texas Hill Country.

Vanderlee Residence
Austin, TX, USA

The restoration of this hillside was accomplished with sixty species of transplanted native plants, flat terraces to retain water and soil, and preserved trees and grasses.

Lea Residence
Austin, TX, USA

A sculpture garden lies nestled among recycled boulders, preserved trees, colorful perennials, and limestone walls. Despite difficult shallow soils, the design achieves a careful layering of colors and textures.

Sesquicentennial Walk, Baylor University
Waco, TX, USA

The Sesquicentennial Walk lies in the heart of Texas' oldest university. The openness of the formal design enhances the connection between four original campus buildings.

Milton Gregory Memorial Garden, Baylor University
Waco, TX, USA

The Moody Library at Baylor houses the sunken Gregory Memorial Garden, where vines, groundcover, and accent trees surround red brick columns and trellises.

J. Robert Anderson, ASLA
Landscape Architect
1715 S. Capitol of Tex. #105
Austin, TX 78746, USA
phone | 512-329-8882
fax | 512-329-8883

CLIENTS

Baylor University

Mrs. Lyndon B. Johnson

Helen Lea

National Cowboy Hall of Fame

National Wildflower Research Center

Pflugerville Independent School District

Schlumberger Well Services

Service Corporation International

Eileen Vanderlee

Andropogon Associates, Ltd.

Andropogon Associates, Ltd. was formed in 1975 to bring an ecological perspective to problem solving in landscape architecture. The firm is now a leader in sustainable design. In master planning and development projects for international, governmental, and institutional landscapes, Andropogon focuses on recognizing existing and potential resources, clarifying purpose, and integrating ecological design strategies.

Andropogon has extensive experience in the adaptive reuse and rehabilitation of historic, urban, and regional sites. The firm has pioneered the restoration and management of natural habitats, from forests to wetlands, in nearly pristine areas to the most disturbed urban and rural environments. Offering a wide range of services in ecological planning and design, Andropogon seeks to produce appropriate solutions that successfully integrate the needs of the client with those of the community and larger environment.

The firm's name was inspired by the common American field grass Andropogon, one of nature's remarkable responses to stress and change in the landscape. Wherever the landscape has been disturbed, Andropogon is one of the first grasses to colonize the ground, providing a self-sustaining cover as native forests gradually return. The economy and elegance with which these grassy meadows heal the wounded landscape aptly express the firm's goals in ecological planning and design. Andropogon Associates, Ltd. seeks to weave together the landscapes of humans and nature for the benefit of both.

Crosby Arboretum
Picayune, MS, USA

Andropogon developed the master plan and landscape design for the Crosby Arboretum, which is dedicated to the preservation, study, and interpretation of plant communities native to the Pearl River Basin on Mississippi's southern coastal plain.

▲
Evoking the feeling of a southern rain-fed swamp, the lake is framed by a canopy of trees and a foreground of rushes, sedges, and aquatic wildflowers. Visitors can view the scene from a boardwalk.

The new Piney Woods Lake adds interest to the arboretum's uniform lowland and provides a dramatic setting for the open-air visitors center designed by Jones and Jennings of Fayetteville, Arkansas.
▼

▲
Through the design of its thematic structure, site plan, interpretive paths, architecture, plant displays, and site management techniques, the arboretum expresses the natural processes and evocative qualities of the Piney Woods.

▲
Fire, a natural management process, was introduced to replicate naturally occurring wildfires that support plants and animals adapted to periodic burning.

This buttercup meadow, a local term for open lowlands where yellow pitcher plants proliferate, was created by habitat management techniques which include burning, species reintroduction, and removal of competing species. ▶

The Woodlands, Central Park
New York City, NY, USA

Andropogon developed a program for the Central Park Conservancy to restore a portion of Frederick Law Olmsted's masterpiece. The plan for the North Woods included restoration of deteriorated historic stonework, pathways, and forest vegetation.

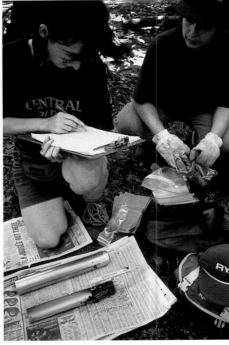

▲
Local school children evaluate the impact of urbanization on soil organisms, which will guide the restoration of native plant communities in the park.

▲
Volunteers remove invasive exotic plants, gather and plant seeds of native species, and form a growing constituency dedicated to park restoration.

▲
On the main path that runs along the Loch, arches, adjacent pools, and cascades, as well as the surrounding forest vegetation, were restored.

▲
New parking areas are designed as a series of nearly level terraces that gently merge into the hillside and are invisible to visitors in the garden below.

The Morris Arboretum of the University of Pennsylvania
Philadelphia, PA, USA

The arboretum is a celebration of the Victorian garden, designed to delight as well as educate the visitor.

As part of the master plan, Andropogon
designed a road that brings visitors to the historic entrance to the site and to a new education
and visitors center.

A series of new paths lead through the restored
Morris gardens, where visitors enjoy restored
historical features and plant collections.

Andropogon Associates, Ltd.
374 Shurs Lane
Philadelphia, PA 19128, USA
phone | 215-487-0700
fax | 215-483-7520

CLIENTS

Central Park Conservancy

Crosby Arboretum

**Morris Arboretum of the
University of Pennsylvania**

Private Residence
Philadelphia, PA, USA

This urban garden enlivens and enriches the
space with a balanced life pool that adds depth
and an element of mystery.

Private Residence
Martha's Vineyard, MA, USA

Designed to create a quiet oasis in a bustling
seaside town, this garden uses the indigenous
plants of the island.

Belt Collins Design Group

In 1953 Robert M. Belt and Walter K. Collins incorporated Belt Collins as a consulting civil engineering and planning firm. Landscape architectural services were added in the late 1950s. The firm's expansion continued with the 1980s addition of Nelson Haworth Golf Course Architects and the recent addition of land surveying and environmental consulting services.

Belt Collins has offices in Hawaii, Singapore, Hong Kong, Australia, Thailand, Malaysia, Guam, the Philippines, and Florida. Stressing the interdependence of its design services, the firm employs approximately 280 personnel. Belt Collins has completed more than eight thousand projects in Hawaii as well as elsewhere in the Pacific Basin, Asia, Africa, Europe, the Middle East, and the mainland United States.

Landscape architectural services include overall conceptual plans for commercial and industrial complexes, parks and recreational areas, and resort and residential communities; street, roadside, and highway corridor landscape plans; nursery programs; exterior signage and hardscape design; outdoor lighting plans; water features design; irrigation plans; and landscape maintenance programs.

Belt Collins works in areas of varying climate and terrain, including the challenging volcanic regions of the Hawaiian Islands. When possible, the firm makes extensive use of available native material and seeks to integrate landscaping with the natural environment.

Out of more than five thousand firms in the United States, the American Society of Landscape Architects' *Landscape Architecture* magazine ranked Belt Collins fifth in terms of revenue. Over the years the firm has been recognized for project excellence, receiving numerous awards for the quality of its landscape architecture.

Mauna Lani Resort
South Kohala, HI, USA

Since 1974 Belt Collins has been involved in planning this major resort and recreation community. The master plan for the 3,000-acre (1,200-hectare) parcel included development strategy, detailed design and infrastructure requirements, the design and construction supervision of two award-winning golf courses, and the preservation of historical sites.

Mauna Kea Resort
South Kohala, HI, USA

In 1962 Belt Collins developed a master plan for the oceanfront Mauna Kea Resort which includes an implementation program for development of a 4,000-acre (1,600-hectare) self-contained luxury resort and recreation community. The continual enhancement of the world-renowned Mauna Kea Beach Hotel and grounds during the past ten years has been a key element of the development plan.

Makaiwa Bay Beach Construction at Mauna Lani Resort
South Kohala, HI, USA

Oceanographic and hydrographic studies were undertaken to establish the engineering feasibility of developing and refurbishing sand beaches at the resort. At the badly eroded beach at Makaiwa Bay, 400 linear feet (120 meters) of artificial beach were added, the slope was increased, and a retaining wall and other support structures were constructed.

Kapalua Resort
Maui, HI, USA

Belt Collins designed the Kapalua Resort master plan for 600 acres (240 hectares) of undeveloped oceanfront land on the northwest coast of Maui, which now includes several hotels, a variety of dwelling types, a resort village, parks and recreation facilities, and three championship eighteen-hole golf courses. Every effort was made to preserve the existing vegetation, beaches, and shoreline. Shown here: Kapalua Golf Villas Multi-Family Development.

Hyatt Singapore Hotel
Singapore

Landscape plan for pool level and all exterior areas, including all hardscape, streams, and waterfalls.

Physical Education and Athletic Facilities, Punahou School
Honolulu, HI, USA

Belt Collins provided master planning, civil and mechanical engineering, and landscape architectural design services for an athletic complex composed of a gymnasium, outdoor track, 167-foot (50-meter) swimming pool, gymnastics and wrestling rooms, handball and basketball courts, weight room and dance studio, tennis courts, locker rooms, and administrative facilities.

Aberdeen Marina Club
Hong Kong

In association with Fox Hawaii, Belt Collins provided complete landscape architectural services for a large marina development on reclaimed land. Features include a children's amusement center, recreation deck, large lawn area, tennis courts, and two swimming pools. Extensive landscaping provides a garden-like setting for both interior and exterior areas.

Surrounded by a landscaped deck, the 248-foot (75-meter) free-form swimming pool includes an 8-foot (2.4-meter) waterfall, water slide leading to a children's pool, and swim-up bar.

Bali Intercontinental
Jimbaran, Indonesia

The Intercontinental is a five-star 450-room beach resort located on a 37-acre (14.8-hectare) site. Belt Collins was responsible for the softscape, hardscape artwork selection, and landscape lighting for the extensive Balinese-inspired landscape design, incorporating formal swimming pools with water spouts and sculptures, fun pools, and natural lagoon areas.

Hyatt Saujana Hotel
Kuala Lumpur, Malaysia

Design of landscape and various water features, including the hotel porte cochère and courtyards.

Shangri-La Hotel
Singapore

From the original hotel in 1968 through three major additions, Belt Collins has provided overall landscape planning, design, and field supervision of all exterior areas, including pathways, water features, swimming pool and terrace layouts, exterior lighting, botanical park, project nursery, and recreational facilities, including a par 3 golf complex.

Island Shangri-La Hotel
Hong Kong

Overall landscape planning for this urban hotel, as well as all the other roof gardens and interior landscape of the entire Pacific Place complex.

Safari Park Hotel
Nairobi, Kenya

Full landscape planning and design services for all external areas including the main entry drive, outdoor restaurants, swimming pools, water features, and water slides were provided. This project received a Design Excellence Award from the Hawaii Chapter of the American Society of Landscape Architects in 1993.

Belt Collins Design Group

680 Ala Moana Boulevard, First Floor
Honolulu, HI 96813-5406, USA
phone | 808-521-5361
fax | 808-538-7819

CLIENTS

Brisbane Airport Authority

Hyatt International

Intercontinental Hotels

Kamehameha Schools / Bernice P. Bishop Estate

Kapalua Land Co. (Maui Land and Pineapple Co.)

Kuok Properties (Shangri-La Hotel Group)

Lend Lease Development / Civil and Civic

Mauna Kea Properties

Mauna Lani Resort

Raffles Hotel Group

Sheraton Hotel Group

State of Hawaii / City and County of Honolulu

Raffles Hotel
Singapore

While this landmark hotel was closed for two years of historic renovation, Belt Collins participated in the design and restoration of the Raffles gardens and courtyards.

Waikapu Sandalwood Golf Course and Waikapu Valley Country Club
Maui, HI, USA

Golf course design for an eighteen-hole golf course and landscape design for two courses and two clubhouses at Waikapu, Maui, was completed by Belt Collins Golfscapes and Nelson & Haworth Golf Course Architects.

A. E. Bye and Janis Hall

A. E. Bye and Janis Hall work with nature in an effort to reveal the core character of a place–its ecology, aesthetic, and spirit. Their commissions range from large private residences to college campuses, parks, and corporations.

Winner of the 1993 American Society of Landscape Architects Medal, among many other prizes, A. E. Bye is known especially for such projects as Gainesway Farm, the Stein bog, the Ridgefield residence, and the Reisley residence. A landscape architect for more than four decades, he is a very accomplished practitioner. Bye is particularly interested in the restoration of native ecologies and in encouraging people to see the mood and unique character of distinct ecosystems, from woodlands to meadows to rocky hillsides and swamps. Since 1951, when he designed the landscape for a Frank Lloyd Wright house in New York using native plants, he has influenced the profession to work responsibly with existing ecological conditions.

Janis Hall is an environmental artist and architect whose years of work in sculpture and architecture shape her work with the landscape. Winner of the 1991 Young Architects Forum Competition, Hall is known for the Mnemonic River, Waterland, Unfurlings, and Murmuring Flow projects. She is particularly interested in the interface between art and nature, where her site-specific sculpture and ecologically sound landscape design work together to create living works of art in living nature. Her work engages natural forces, such as light, shadow, wind, and water flow, in an effort to counterpoise ephemeral phenomena with the immutable elements of a place. Hall's early design (from 1985 through 1986) at Mnemonic River, a project that dynamically reveals the phenomena of light and shadow, has been highly influential.

Both Bye and Hall combine design with teaching. They have lectured and exhibited their photographs of their work at galleries and universities across the United States.

Stallion Barn Complex, Gainesway Farm
Lexington, KY, USA

Bye designed the landscape around the new stallion barns at Gainesway Farm, a serene place characterized by gently rolling land in the heart of bluegrass country. The approach, developed in collaboration with architect Theodore M. Ceraldi, preserves the atmosphere of the surrounding meadows. The barns were spaced loosely together, avoiding the rigidity of an orthogonal layout and allowing them to be slightly offset from one another.

The planning concept takes into account the needs of the horses and the owner's desire for majestic trees such as beech and yellowwood. Trees were placed far enough apart from each other to allow substantial growth over time. A 172-foot-long (52-meter-long) water trough is at the center of the complex, located under an existing double row of oaks. The jets of water were kept deliberately low in order to avoid exciting the thoroughbreds.

A. E. Bye and Janis Hall 31

Private Residence
Ridgefield, CT

To create a place that celebrates the native condition, Bye worked closely with an existing woody, rocky promontory where twisted and jagged chestnut oaks and heavy masses of mountain laurel dominated the scene. He designed the landscape primarily by removing plants that were not indigenous, prevented access for people, were overgrown, or obstructed the growth of other plants.

The project required Bye to determine, often by climbing through thickets, the nature and location of existing vegetation. The balance of solid and void was carefully considered as the confinements of narrow paths created through the lush mountain laurel were contrasted to the open glades. The forest floor was respected, with its profusion of mosses, lichens, ferns, Canada mayflowers, and trilliums. Bye allowed some fallen branches and decaying trees to remain on the site, affirming that they are as much a part of the forest as live plants.

Murmuring Flow (Site-Specific Sculpture), Private Residence
Southwestern Connecticut, USA

In a section of Connecticut characterized by rolling hills, rock outcroppings, streams, and ponds, Hall designed a landscape that augments the site's existing character and, through the creation of a site-specific sculpture, introduces a sense of flowing water.

Although no water actually flows in the dry, rocky stream, the sound of trickling water is implied in the sculpture. Hall connected the interior of an old walled garden adjacent to a Georgian house to the wilder landscape beyond the walls by introducing two streams, one of yew, one of stone, that well up like springs out of the earth and then entwine before flowing along two opposite walls. The rolling, undulating ribbon of yew breaks through a garden gate and flows along the front of the house for 150 feet (45 meters). The stream of boulders and field-stone breaks through a transparent gate and, for 300 feet (90 meters), engages the terrace behind the house, the lawn, and the hanging branches of an old spruce tree before ending near the edge of the woods.

Summer Evening

Mnemonic River, Private Residence
Southeastern Massachusetts

Hall designed a landscape that blends seamlessly into the broader context by incorporating parts of the surrounding environment: wildflowers, native plants, sculpted earth, light, shadow, wind, and water, both real and imaginary. She sculpted the earth behind the house into the form of a dry riverbed, visually echoing the bay and distant hill. As the sun rises and falls, light and shadow is revealed on the undulating earth, transforming the landscape.

Hall's grading is intended to abstract the materiality of the earth, revealing that which is immutable about the place and making palpable the earth's primal character. The earth becomes soft and alternately warm, like glowing embers, or cool, like water. Throughout her work, Hall recognizes that the earth is not the only primary substance. In this project, for instance, the seeming immateriality of the air is transformed into an active, volatile presence. By incorporating the play of light and shadow in her design, she engages the fleeting and ephemeral, and contrasts it with the immutable.

Spring Afternoon

Winter Morning

Autumn Evening

Autumn Morning

A. E. Bye and Janis Hall
300 Central Park West
New York, NY 10024, USA
phone | 212-873-4615
fax | 212-873-4615

CLIENTS

Bernheim Forest, Arboretum and Nature Preserve

The Cooper Union for the Advancement of Science and Art

Mr. and Mrs. John Gaines

Gainesway Farm

Harvey Hubbell Corporation

Lafayette College

Mr. and Mrs. Leonard Lauder

Mr. and Mrs. Alfred R. Shands III

Dean Cardasis and Associates

As a theoretician as well as practitioner, Dean Cardasis designs projects that are a sophisticated expression of important contemporary ideas in landscape architecture. But far from being elite aesthetic experiments, his creations are decidedly human-oriented places, ranging from shady and contemplative personal strolling gardens, to whimsical playgrounds for children, to celebratory public gathering spaces. His firm specializes in private gardens, as well as public parks and plazas.

Cardasis' design responds to existing qualities of a site that often are overlooked. Hence, a horse chestnut branch, the patterns of light on the ground, or the way snow falls, for example, are redefined and illuminated by the purposeful way he organizes space. New expressions of gateways, allées, and outdoor rooms are formed by combining existing site features with both traditional and sometimes surprising contemporary materials originally intended for other purposes.

For one project, Cardasis designed an arbor from climbing rope for vines, rather than people, to climb. For a teacher's garden, he made pool copings from salvaged blackboard pieces. By imaginatively interweaving contemporary cultural materials with existing site features, indigenous plants, dimension lumber, and native stone, Cardasis' landscapes reveal their sites in inventive and contextual ways.

Cardasis often practices a form of design/build, which allows for spontaneous improvisation with the land and a more direct and continuous relationship with his clients. This method adds vitality to the finished works, which are useful, imaginative, inspiring, and sometimes humorous expressions of both the sites and his clients.

In addition to being a practicing landscape architect, Dean Cardasis is a professor at the University of Massachusetts, Amherst, and director of the James Rose Center in Ridgewood, New Jersey.

Durfee Gardens
Amherst, MA, USA

At what once was a small New England land grant college, Durfee Gardens organizes five interlocking contemporary spaces according to the historic agricultural principle of the grid, making a park which is a garden.

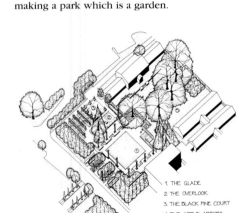

1. THE GLADE
2. THE OVERLOOK
3. THE BLACK PINE COURT
4. THE APPLE ARBORS
5. THE MEDITATION GARDEN

▲
The organizing grid of the garden is revealed in this wintry expression of the orchard, where snow-laden allées made by Kevlar cord will support apple trees and define a series of connecting pathways.

◄ Spontaneous improvisations such as this composition of tree branches and stone specimens are back-lit by the morning sun seen through fiberglass screens after a snowfall.

Eleven 18-foot tall (5.5-meter-tall) trellis/columns made of wood, red Kevlar cord, and fluorescent Plexiglas sheathing help articulate the spaces and illuminate the college landscape.

Durfee Gardens
Amherst, MA, USA

Where once was a parking lot, a new conservatory entry courtyard and overlook are defined by native stones and existing and indigenous plantings; including beech, birch, and mountain laurel. ▶

▲
An existing horse chestnut and rhododendrons are composed with Fiberglass and wood screens to create a simple and elegant gateway to the meditation grove.

▲
The quality of light passing through Fiberglass screens adds texture to stone paving made from local river cobbles and mountain schist.

◀ The Glade is an open, sunny, celebratory gathering place containing ten types of turf grasses as well as more than forty species of perennials along its borders.

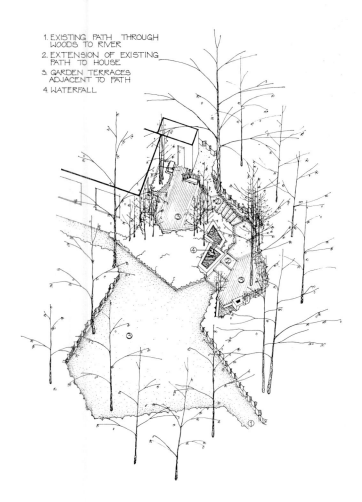

1. EXISTING PATH THROUGH
   WOODS TO RIVER
2. EXTENSION OF EXISTING
   PATH TO HOUSE
3. GARDEN TERRACES
   ADJACENT TO PATH
4. WATERFALL

A Strolling Garden
Shutesbury, MA, USA

This garden extends an existing woodland path directly to the client's back door, thus completing an important connection to a nearby river. Irregular terraces along the path provide "rooms" for outdoor living.

The path sidles past a great white pine. Cobble-size stones dug up in re-grading are woven with existing plant materials to help achieve a character that is distinctive yet of the place.
▼

A geomorphic white cedar deck along the path is integrated into the site by using existing pine seedlings and the canopy of a single existing oak as its edges.
▲

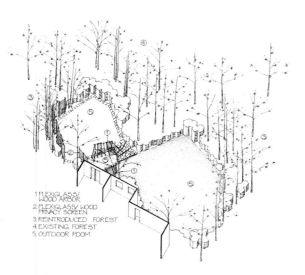

A Plastic Garden
Northampton, MA, USA

Colorful plastic panels whimsically extend the white vinyl siding of a typical subdivision house to meet a reintroduced forest edge. A series of three unique garden rooms results, providing a stimulating play space for children and adults.

▲
Assembled as if from so many pick-up sticks, standard dimension lumber creates screens, decks, and arbors that divide the space and provide a framework for light-transforming plastic panels.

▲
A privacy screen made of wood and colorful translucent and transparent Plexiglas reveals a shoji-like silhouette of surrounding trees.

▲
As part of an irregular overhead structure, transparent blue Plexiglas polarizes light and redefines the sky.

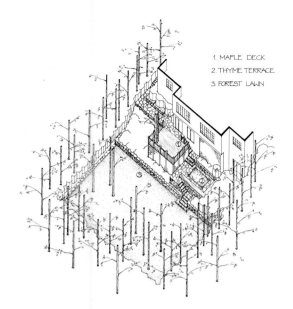

1. MAPLE DECK
2. THYME TERRACE
3. FOREST LAWN

A Kettle Hole Garden
Amherst, MA, USA

On the site of an ancient kettle hole, a series of rectilinear terraces was designed to connect the interior spaces of a newly sited house to the kettle hole floor and surrounding woodland.

As viewed from a bedroom balcony, the garden ▶ spaces include a cedar deck, thyme terrace, and forest lawn.

The thyme terrace includes several cultivars of ▶ creeping thyme whose flowering seasons overlap, prolonging bloom and creating a shifting mosaic of color and texture.

By extending the rectilinear geometry of the garden into the woodland and carefully clearing some of the vegetation, the basin has been transformed into a place where garden and woodland meet.
▼

Dean Cardasis and Associates
32 Cosby Avenue
Amherst, MA 01002, USA
phone | 413-549-4937
fax | 413-548-8825

Carrick Design Inc.

Founded in 1985, architectural landscape firm Carrick Design has gained an international reputation for the design and remodeling of more than fifty golf courses, golf course communities, and resorts of exceptional beauty and variety.

The Toronto-based firm's expertise has evolved through many years of hands-on involvement with the total planning, design, and construction supervision of a wide spectrum of work. With experience in many settings and countries, the firm has handled projects of varied complexity and scale.

Doug Carrick believes that every golf course should have its own design character, so he blends the specific requirements of each project with the unique attributes of the site. His core design philosophy is rooted in the traditional values of the game of golf and in his dedication to developing fresh new concepts for each project. His golf courses offer visual interest and definition, while each hole blends seamlessly with the natural flow of the terrain. For all levels of players, Carrick designs courses that offer memorable game challenges, variety, playability, and exciting shot values.

King Valley Golf Club
King City, Ontario, Canada

Golf Digest ranked this exclusive private club near Toronto as Canada's Second Best New Course in 1991. A sensitive, classic design and carefully planned construction process preserved the site's mature natural character. King Valley offers a stern challenge from the championship tees and excellent playability from the regular tee positions.

Angus Glen Golf Club
Markham, Ontario, Canada

A truly world-class public course and highly
regarded corporate tournament facility near
Toronto, Angus Glen was named Canada's Best
New Course in 1995 by *Golf Digest* magazine.
The design is on a grand, spacious scale, with
wide rolling fairways and deeply sculpted
bunkers that blend harmoniously with the
surrounding countryside.

This unique public golf facility developed in
one of Canada's national parks opened in 1991.
Designed to successfully deal with sensitive
environmental factors, Twin Rivers integrates
interesting golf course features with a spectacular wilderness setting alongside two white-water
salmon rivers tumbling to the nearby
Atlantic Ocean.

Greystone Golf Club
Milton, Ontario, Canada

A private club on the edge of the scenic Niagara Escarpment just west of Toronto, Greystone sensitively integrates the natural features of the course's picturesque setting and rolling terrain. This course has earned an enviable reputation for its challenging yet playable layout.

Osprey Valley Heathlands Golf Club
Caledon, Ontario, Canada

A public course opened in 1993, the Osprey
Valley Heathlands Golf Club takes its inspiration from the traditional links courses of
Scotland and England. To maximize the variety
of shots, the formerly flat site was sculpted
with dune-like hills, undulating fairways, pot
bunkers, and bentgrass hollows.

CLIENTS

Capilano Golf and Country Club

Clublink Corporation

Gates of Markham Developments Ltd.

Intrawest Corp.

Magna International

The Mandarin Club of Toronto

Oakdale Golf and Country Club

Osprey Valley Partnership

The Park Country Club of Buffalo

Parks Canada

St. George's Golf and Country Club

Carrick Design Inc.
255 Duncan Mill Road, Suite 302
Don Mills, Ontario M3B 3H9, Canada
phone | 416-447-6295
fax | 416-447-6334

Design Workshop, Inc.

For more than twenty-five years, Design Workshop has aspired to plan and design great places that people remember–places that bring people closer to their environment.

Sometimes the scope of planning these places is very broad, such as when the firm develops master plans for counties, new communities, urban centers, and resorts. At other times the work focuses on detailed design for public parks, residences, and roadways. Technology always plays an important role. Design Workshop continually searches for new tools to improve its mapping and presentation capabilities, so people can learn more about the land and make better decisions about its use.

Another common thread among the firm's efforts is its commitment to conserving natural landscapes. Projects begin with a thorough study of environmental–as well as cultural and historic–resources, so that rather than pushing preconceived notions onto the land, the design protects and plays off significant natural features.

Design Workshop believes that the best way to achieve solid stewardship of the environment is to involve the community in the design and planning process. This approach presents the chance to merge diverse, even conflicting priorities into a common vision, and it educates citizens about the value of their natural spaces.

Design Workshop has been guided by these principles since it was founded in 1969 as a two-person firm in Aspen, Colorado. Now it is an international award-winning firm with offices in Aspen, Denver, and Vail, Colorado; Phoenix, Arizona; Albuquerque and Santa Fe, New Mexico; Jackson Hole, Wyoming; Lake Tahoe, California; and São Paulo, Brazil. To every new landscape, Design Workshop brings the same goal: creating places that bring people and the environment together–to the benefit of both.

Aguas Claras Community
Belo Horizonte, Brazil

At Aguas Claras, Design Workshop created a plan to transform a soon-to-be-closed iron ore mine into a new mountain community above the metropolis of Belo Horizonte. The approach includes working with operations planners while the mine is still functioning so mining by-products can be managed to have less impact on future uses of the land.

Alexander Valley Vineyards
Alexander River Valley, CA, USA

To minimize disturbance to views, Design
Workshop's plan for residential sites on this
scenic vineyard estate relied on a careful visual
analysis. A three-dimensional computer modeling
program was used to validate the analysis and
illustrate how new homes would complement
the landscape.

Little Nell Hotel
Aspen, CO, USA

The award-winning Little Nell Hotel site design harmonizes public access to the Aspen Mountain ski area with private spaces for hotel guests. Streets were eliminated, giving preference to people over cars, and the town is now connected to the ski area by a pedestrian plaza adjacent to the hotel.

Western Area Power Association Operations and Maintenance Center
Phoenix, AZ, USA

WAPA needed to consolidate its regional offices into one energy-efficient headquarters. Design Workshop developed the layout of roadways, parking, walks, a retention basin, and landscaping for the site. Environmentally sensitive desert landscaping replaced the existing oasis landscaping, conserving water and energy resources.

Bow Canmore Visual Assessment
Bow Valley, Alberta, Canada

The beautiful Bow River Valley Corridor has
experienced intense pressure for new developments, ranging from golf courses and resorts to
an aerial tramway. Using sophisticated computer
capabilities, Design Workshop prepared an
award-winning simulation of the visual impacts
of development.

Hills Park, Summerlin Community
Las Vegas, NV, USA

Hills Park is the visual centerpiece and prime
gathering place for the Summerlin community in
Las Vegas. The park sports a southwestern theme
and provides a venue for numerous recreational,
cultural, and educational activities. Special features include an urban plaza and performing
arts amphitheater.

Design Workshop, Inc.
1390 Lawrence Street, Suite 200
Denver, CO 80204, USA
phone | 303-623-5186
fax | 303-623-2260

CLIENTS

Aspen Ski Company

**The Conservation Fund, Boulder,
Colorado**

**Cottle Graybeal Yaw Architects,
Aspen, Colorado**

**Howard Hughes Properties,
Summerlin, Las Vegas, Nevada**

**Intrawest Development Corporation,
Vancouver, British Columbia**

SBW, Seoul, Korea

**Snowmass Land Company, Snowmass,
Colorado**

**Trillium Corporation, Denver,
Colorado**

**U.S. Fish & Wildlife Service,
Washington, D.C.**

Winter Park Recreational Association,

Roger DeWeese Inc. and Associates (RDI&A)

Roger DeWeese Inc. and Associates (RDI&A) is concerned with long-term aesthetic and physical project success through collaborative design that has a sense of timelessness. RDI&A resists the inclination to explore preconceived notions, concentrating instead on listening to and understanding its clients' objectives.

Over the last twenty-five years RDI&A has enjoyed a diverse practice mainly in the southwestern United States, which also has extended south to Georgia, east to Rhode Island, and north to Wyoming. Project types include the planning and design of corporate developments, shopping centers, resorts, regional and local parks, municipal complexes, military facilities, housing, private residences, restaurants, medical buildings, churches, schools, and marinas. RDI&A has received more than sixty-five awards for design excellence.

Success for RDI&A has many facets. Social success often is expressed by the public's physical and emotional response to the created environment. For the client, expectations must be met or exceeded. Physically, the improvements need to be of sufficient quality to last for more than a reasonable time period without unanticipated maintenance and repair costs. For this reason, RDI&A emphasizes the importance of proper engineering, construction, and maintenance. Quite simply, the project has to work.

RDI&A believes design should inspire people to experience the project. The elements of surprise and mystery heighten the user experience. Predictable and trendy design based on matrices and obscure metaphors are avoided. Additional richness results from playing one element against another, such as contrasting formal against informal, rough against polished textures, light against dark, and placid against active.

The real challenge in design is to create the most with the least and, in those rare instances where budget is not limited, to exercise enough restraint to keep the main design concept from becoming diluted. In all of its work, RDI&A emphasizes the importance of understanding and respecting the past before exploring the future.

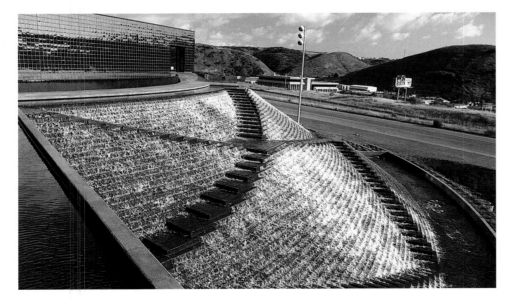

Wateridge Marketing Pavilion
San Diego, CA, USA

The design of the water feature was an exercise in restraint to avoid overpowering the elegantly simple glass block building. The water feature was approached as if it were a large earth sculpture. Black concrete was used to contrast with the aerated white water.

The "steps" were intended for future use to connect the pedestrian access from the pavilion to the public transportation system at the intersection below. Pond areas were plumbed for drains in case water conservation measures or prohibitive power costs require their future conversion into planters.

The focus of the front entrance is the pavilion itself, accented by a quiet stainless steel sculpture. A semicircular row of palm trees is reflected in the pond and serves as the transition element between the informal arrival landscape and the formal pavilion/waterscape.

The pavilion commands visual significance from adjacent freeways and serves as the marketing center and gateway to the 125-acre (50-hectare) Wateridge Corporate Business Park. The formality of the glass block building and water feature contrasts significantly with the intentionally informal park-like entry setting.

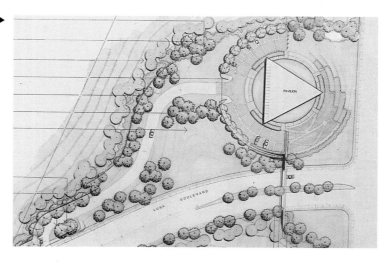

Stonecrest
San Diego, CA, USA

Originally an aggregate quarry, Stonecrest's 318-acre (127-hectare) site presented many physical and planning challenges. The master planning included relocating riparian and wetland habitat, preserving open space, connecting to mass transit and other pedestrian/bicycle systems, and soil reclamation.

The quadrangular interior courtyard is approached beneath a concrete and steel overhead structure that provides a pedestrian scale at the ground plane beneath the multi-story buildings. The illusion of pond depth was created by subtly stepping the bottom with increasingly dark granite tile that is black at the deepest level. ▶

The quadrangular courtyard provides a different environment from each of the four main access points. Subtle elevation differentials provide the opportunity for adequate drainage and elevated sitting areas that command a view of the surroundings. Curved terrazzo benches complement the curvilinear forms of the walls and water feature. ▶

Equidon Plaza at Wateridge
San Diego, CA, USA

Water is the main connection between all groups of buildings on this 125-acre (50-hectare) project. The project design guidelines require links from the exterior spaces to the interior courtyards through the use of various water elements.

▲
Axial water runnels accented by rows of palms were used to make the transition between the exterior and interior courtyard pedestrian spaces. The reflectivity of the buildings amplifies the visual illusion of greater space.

▲
A 30-foot (9-meter) elevation differential between the upper and lower motor courts became a visual and physical adventure while transitioning the courtyard. Blocks of slate were used from the same quarry as the building slate to blend architecture with landscape architecture in the cascading water feature.

▲
While the courtyard can accommodate large special events, it also serves as a quiet retreat and divorces its users from the scale of the surrounding buildings. The interior facing offices also become as leasable as those with exterior views.

Uptown
San Diego, CA, USA

This thirteen-acre mixed-use in-fill project incorporates 320 residential units and 140,000 square feet (12,600 square meters) of office and retail space. Primary objectives were to complement the surrounding older neighborhoods' architectural vernacular and create a subtle transition between the project's residential and commercial areas.

One of many entrances to the residential area. ▶

▲
One of the street scenes that provides a friendly interface with the existing adjacent neighborhood.

Roger DeWeese Inc. and Associates (RDI&A)
13140 Carousel Lane
Del Mar, CA 92014, USA
phone | 619-794-9991
fax | 619-794-9998

CLIENTS

American Nevada Corporation

Daniel Realty Corporation

Guarantee Service Corporation

Home Capital Corporation

La Jolla Development Company

Lorimer and Case for Odmark Thelan

Melvin Simon and Associates

City and County of San Diego

Teleklew Productions

University of California

The space within the project expands to reveal large open park areas for passive recreation. ▶

du Toit Allsopp Hillier

The goal of the members of the du Toit Allsopp Hillier partnership is to engage in the creative design of human habitats that work well and uplift the spirit.

Much of North America's existing designed environment does not meet this goal. People travel long distances to visit wonderful environments, but rarely do they live or work in them. The firm strives to be an agent for change, increasing rather than reducing the number of well designed environments available to people in their everyday lives.

This endeavor requires interdisciplinary effort. The firm contributes three of the needed design disciplines: landscape architecture, urban planning, and building architecture, which often are combined as urban design. In most of the firm's projects, the interdisciplinary requirements are much broader, requiring the firm to collaborate

with a wide range of environmental, engineering, and economic specialists to ensure a balanced, multidimensional perspective.

The effort to create an environment that works well and encourages a sense of well-being usually means preserving the best of what already exists. In each project the firm tries to understand and document the essence of the place, both its assets and liabilities, and to use this understanding as a starting point for the design interventions.

While the firm's range is wide–from small private gardens to large public areas such as the grounds of Canada's Parliament–most of the partnership's work involves connective landscapes: the uniting spaces of a university campus; the streetscape of an arterial road; or the linked streets, lanes, and squares of an urban center.

St. Patrick Escarpment,
Confederation Boulevard,
The National Capital
Ottawa, Ontario, Canada

Roadway, bicycle route, and pedestrian esplanade leading to Major's Hill Park.

View north along the esplanade to Alexandra ▶ Bridge and Hull, Quebec.

University of Windsor Campus Plan
Windsor, Ontario, Canada

View through portico of academic building to campus bookstore and forecourt.

Business School and bookstore forecourt; academic green to left.

▼

Sixteen Mile Creek Bridge
Oakville, Ontario, Canada

As part of a larger landscape design for a new arterial road crossing the Sixteen Mile Creek, the firm designed the bridge railings, overlooks, and other bridge finishes as input to the engineering works.

Confederation Square
The National Capital
Ottawa, Ontario, Canada

The reconstruction of Confederation Square, home of Canada's primary war memorial, clarifies the triangular configuration of the space; better accommodates public ceremonies; and improves the safety, comfort, and enjoyment of users. This is an aerial perspective of the concept proposal.

Illustration: Gordon Grice & Associates

Detail studies of rehabilitation concept.
▼

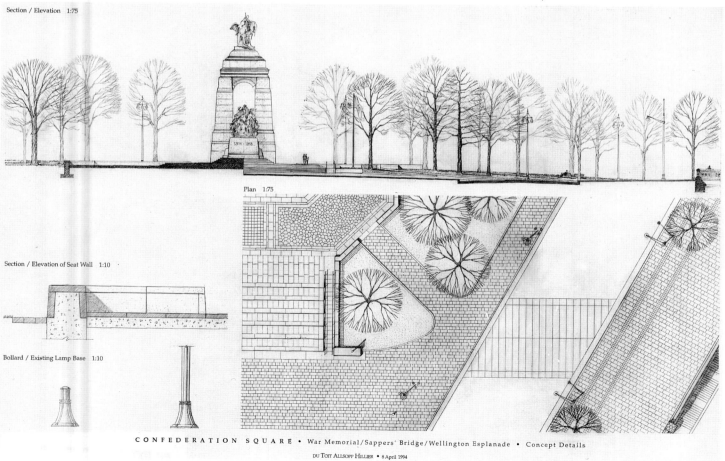

Section / Elevation 1:75

Plan 1:75

Section / Elevation of Seat Wall 1:10

Bollard / Existing Lamp Base 1:10

CONFEDERATION SQUARE • War Memorial/Sappers' Bridge/Wellington Esplanade • Concept Details

DU TOIT ALLSOPP HILLIER • 8 April 1994

Illustration: John Hillier

Gooderham & Worts
Toronto, Ontario, Canada

The landscape plan for redeveloping the Gooderham & Worts nineteenth-century distillery complex reinforces and extends the existing tight network of streets, lanes, and courts to integrate historic buildings and new development, interpret the site's natural and industrial heritage, and provide opportunities for festive market and recreation attractions.

Illustration: Gordon Grice & Associates

du Toit Allsopp Hillier
50 Park Road, Toronto
Ontario M4W 2N5, Canada
phone | 416-968-9479
fax | 416-968-0687

CLIENTS

Allied Domecq Pension Funds

National Capital Commission

Town of Oakville, Ontario

Public Works Canada

Toronto Transit Commission

University of Windsor

Spadina/LRT Streetscape Design Study
Toronto, Ontario, Canada

The streetscape design for Spadina Avenue Light Rapid Transit corridor provides for a central streetcar median, pedestrian shelters, trees, decorative paving, lighting, signage, and public art. The view shown is looking south from the university toward Lake Ontario.

EDSA/Edward D. Stone, Jr. & Associates, Inc.

EDSA is a full-service planning and landscape architecture firm with a far-reaching international practice and reputation. As one of the largest U.S.-based firms of its kind, EDSA has the resources to manage diverse planning and design challenges for public and private sector clients. Serving both domestic markets and the global development community, the firm works effectively in remote locations and diverse cultures.

The landscape architects at EDSA are concerned with the long-term welfare of the communities and environments in which they work. As a professional service organization, the firm is committed to clients' success. Offering guidance in balancing land use with the natural environment, EDSA is dedicated to excellence in design and client services, a commitment that has continued for more than thirty-seven years.

The firm is widely recognized for its abilities to deal with complex projects. EDSA's experience has evolved in four key market sectors: new community planning, hotels and resorts, themed attractions, and high-profile public sector projects.

Port de Plaisance
Saint Maarten, Netherlands Antilles

El Conquistador
Fajardo, Puerto Rico

Las Casitas
Fajardo, Puerto Rico

Port de Plaisance
Saint Martin, Netherlands Antilles

Atlantis
Paradise Island, Bahamas

Atlantis
Paradise Island, Bahamas

Hyatt Regency Aruba
Oranjestad, Aruba

Hyatt Regency Aruba
Oranjestad, Aruba

Grand Cypress Resort
Orlando, FL, USA

EDSA

**Edward D. Stone, Jr.
& Associates, Inc.**
1512 E. Broward Boulevard
Suite #110
Fort Lauderdale, FL 33301, USA
phone | 954-524-3330
fax | 954-524-0177

Grissim/Metz Associates, Inc.

Grissim/Metz Associates has followed sound and simple principles since its inception more than thirty years ago. The firm's success arises from a creative design approach combined with total involvement in each project from concept through construction.

A diversity of clientele and projects makes up the GMA portfolio. Types of projects include shopping centers, parks and recreational facilities, universities, urban design, industrial projects, hospitals, residences, office buildings, housing, and municipal facilities.

The firm's services include site planning and design, hardscape and landscape planning and design, and golf course design. Grissim/Metz supports its design efforts with a solid understanding of construction methods and detailing, developed through the professional staff's more than one hundred years of collective experience. Dedication to the highest design and construction standards has brought the firm national recognition and more than thirty-five design awards.

Designer: John N. Grissim

The Gardens Shopping Center
West Palm Beach Gardens, FL, USA

The landscape of The Gardens complements the Addison Mizner style of architecture established in Palm Beach, Florida. Gateways, organized planting arrangements, and tropical plant materials are key to the design. The main entrance features decorative paving and mature Canary Island palm trees.

The mall entrance, where large plant material ▶ and extensive bed plantings create an outdoor environment consistent with the concept of The Gardens.

Designer: John N. Grissim

Designer: John N. Grissim

Windemere Residential Development
Grosse Pointe Farms, MI, USA

A single-family residential development occupies the site where the estate of Henry Ford II once stood. Naturalistic landscaping, privacy screening, and classic residential streetscape treatments provide a traditional Grosse Pointe Farms neighborhood character. This view is of the community building.

View of typical streetscape treatment.
▼

Designer: John N. Grissim

Regent Court Office Building, Ford Land Development
Dearborn, MI, USA

The auto court/plaza was conceived as a space to be viewed from various levels. Bold patterns, complementary warm colors, and selected plant material modulate scale, provide texture, add seasonal interest, and invite human interaction. . The surface evolves into undulating three-dimensional brick and grass ribbons, emphasizing depth and shadow, providing perspective, and creating a sense of motion.

Designer: Randall K. Metz

Designer: Randall K. Metz

Designer: Randall K. Metz

▲
Ground level view of courtyard.

▲
View of the courtyard in the evening with ginkgo trees in fall color highlighted by ground-mounted accent lighting.

Somerset Collection
Troy, MI, USA

The landscape surrounding this renovated shopping center enhances the architecture without competing with it. Shown here: a view of the grand court from the exterior.

Designers: John N. Grissim, C. Carey Baker.

◀ Parking areas are screened and modulated by broad strokes of similar plant material, accented by more than twenty-two thousand annual flowers. The simple yet effective use of the plant material creates an outdoor environment consistent with the architectural elegance of the center.

Designers: John N. Grissim, Randall K. Metz, Marc R. Russell

Riverfront Plaza
Lansing, MI, USA

The design concept for the plaza was a simple arc, reflecting the shape of the Grand River and new convention center. The result is a linear park adjacent to the river, visually and physically integrated with the contextual architecture and site. The new promenade walkway, together with the plaza, amphitheater, gazebo/band shelter, and festival spaces provide the city with a multifunctional park catering to private and public events, including the popular annual "Riverfest."

View of fountain with custom railing along river's edge.
▼

▲
View from Michigan Avenue overpass of plaza adjacent to the river.

Designers: Marc R. Russell, Randall K. Metz

CLIENTS

Chrysler Corporation

Detroit Parks and Recreation Dept.

Forbes/Cohen Properties, Inc.

Ford Motor Company

General Motors Corporation

Kelly Services

Kenneth Neumann/Joel Smith
Architects, Inc.

Minoru Yamasaki and Associates, Inc.

Oakland University, Michigan

Rossetti Associates, Inc.

Sea World of Florida

Sea World of Ohio

Shepley, Bulfinch, Richardson &
Abbott, Architects, Inc.

The Taubman Company, Inc.

TMP Associates, Inc.

Designers: John N. Grissim, Paul R. Andriese

Private Residence
Bloomfield, MI, USA

View to front door with triple rows of Bradford pear trees along the driveway, architecturally aligned with the house. A granite-block arrival court is the terminus of the drive and forecourt to the formal entrance of the house designed by Hugh Newell Jacobson.

Grissim/Metz Associates
37801 Twelve Mile Road
Farmington Hills, MI 48331, USA
phone | 810-553-2500
fax | 810-553-2505

Olmsted and the Twentieth-Century Park

Frederick Law Olmsted was a young and unknown park department employee when, in 1857, he collaborated with architect Calvert Vaux on the design competition for Central Park. Their winning entry, the Greensward Plan, was a romantic landscape with scenic vistas, still lakes, green meadows, and woodlands that began a park tradition that continues today. The development of the Park was carefully conceived and artfully constructed from 840 acres (336 hectares) of swampy land with rock outcroppings. It was a monumental undertaking in terms of both engineering and cost.

Olmsted considered his urban landscapes to be both works of art and experiments in democracy. People of all social classes could mingle together and find relief from the congestion and unrelenting pace of New York City. The success of Central Park started a public parks movement in the United States as cities and towns across the nation clamored for a Central Park of their own. Despite his success, Olmsted's revolutionary and innovative visions were often criticized and frustrated by political maneuvering.

Following Olmsted's retirement, New York City parks suffered greatly from neglect. By the 1930s there were only 119 playgrounds for a city that contained nearly 1,700,000 children under the age of twelve, which equals one playground for every 14,000 children. What the city called a playground was often an unpaved vacant lot equipped with little more than a slide or swing and chicken wire strung around it. "Children's gardens" in playgrounds were the only places where inner-city kids could engage in the activity of digging. Children would wait in long lines with their pails and shovels until a spot in the "garden" was open.

Robert Moses took over the Parks Department in 1934 as the first citywide parks commissioner. Moses was a reformer and a builder, a man with far-reaching authority and influence. With the help of federal relief work funds, Moses hired tens of thousands of laborers and constructed hundreds of new playgrounds around the city. In contrast to Olmsted, Moses treated parks principally as recreational facilities. Natural parks were consequently misused and overused, which led to the deterioration of their landscapes. Moses, whose negative effects on the city are well chronicled, nonetheless nearly tripled the size of the parks system by the time he retired in 1960.

During most of the 1970s New Yorkers watched their parks and playgrounds rapidly decay as a growing financial crisis resulted in massive budget cuts. The parks system that Moses built was too vast to be maintained in such a period of fiscal constraint. Even Central Park and Prospect Park in Brooklyn (often considered Olmsted's masterpiece) were not spared. Projects under construction stopped.

The Greensward Plan of Central Park, ca. 1857

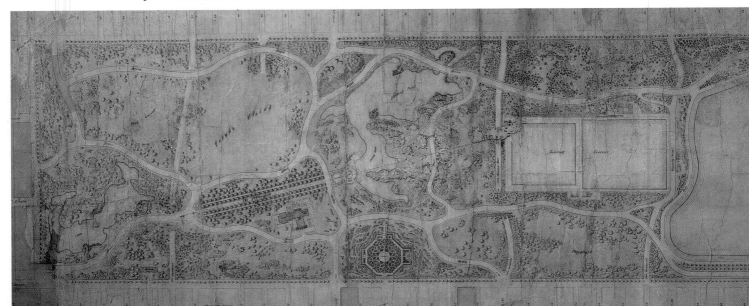

Communities were left to fend for their parks themselves. The city eventually solved its fiscal problems, but the damage had already been done. Many of the great public parks were dangerous places left in a state of ruin.

Yet what emerged during the 1980s may be considered the beginning a new era of parks and recreation design in New York City. The landscape architectural community saw this time as an opportunity to reconstruct the parks system based on principles of the ecology and preservation movements that were sweeping the nation. A renewed emphasis was placed on stewardship of the existing historic parks. The legacy left by Olmsted and Vaux, particularly Central Park, was recognized as not just an amenity, but the very heart and soul of the city itself.

Wetlands were restored, wildlife habitats were protected, historic houses underwent renovations, and playgrounds were fitted with new play equipment accessible to all children. Planning and design tactics were instituted to assure that these vast cultural and ecological resources would be protected, preserved, and restored for future generations.

Today New York City has by far the largest urban park network in the United States. It includes more than 26,000 acres (10,400 hectares) — nearly fifteen percent of the city's total area—and is made up of parks and playgrounds, recreation centers, urban plazas, monuments, historic houses, wetlands, and even a working farm. Parks and recreation design follows a long tradition of innovation, combining new technology with ecological principles. It is a heritage that began with the design and engineering strategies employed by Olmsted and Vaux more than 100 years ago. These parks were state-of-the-art then—ecologically sensitive—and could still be considered state-of-the-art now. One recent study of the Ravine in Prospect Park, for example, revealed that the cascades were designed to be not just aesthetically pleasing, but to catch siltation and help filter the water.

Queens Farm Museum
Little Neck, New York USA

Twin Islands Salt Marsh
Bronx, New York USA

One of the goals today is to improve park ecosystems and the way people experience them. Consequently, parks are not always preserved or returned to their original states. The vast amounts of ornamental plantings once installed by Olmsted have long since vanished. Woodlands have emerged in their place through the process of natural selection. In the name of ecological sustainability, native seeds are collected and propagated, and saplings planted to enhance and promote the existing woodlands.

Although there is a vocabulary of materials and details expressed in the parks that is unique to New York City (concrete and wood slat benches, Central Park lighting fixtures, iron fencing, hexagonal block pavers made from asphalt), new details are developed to meet contemporary standards and needs, yet still fit into an historic park setting. A new cast iron drinking fountain that is wheelchair accessible is one recent example.

New York City parks and playgrounds receive an intensity of use seldom found elsewhere. Many manufacturers use these environments as testing laboratories for new materials and products. The first safety surfacing used in the United States was tested and installed in a New York City playground. Today children don't have to wait in long, hopeless lines to engage in some of their favorite activities. New concepts about recreation and play have led to playground designs with themes that are based on context or local historical events. Other notions have produced science playgrounds, imagination playgrounds, and musical playgrounds.

Mt. Prospect Park
Brooklyn, New York USA

Olmsted's vision of urban parks—a synthesis of nature and the city—continues to be seen in the restoration of the historic parks. However, what is emerging instead of a strict historic restoration is a blend of materials and details historically appropriate to different periods in each park, a landscape grounded in ecological principles, and uses that reflect the habits of twentieth-century urban residents. A clear interpretation of this new type of hybrid park—a park that is like nothing Olmsted and Vaux could ever have imagined—has yet to appear.

Arthur Kleinman, ASLA

Manhattan Beach
(Pat Parlato) Playground
Brooklyn, New York USA

Grupo de Diseño Urbano

Mario Schjetnan and Jose Luis Perez of Grupo de Diseño Urbano are recognized for their integration of the concepts of environmental design, connecting architecture, landscape, and city to create unified and continuous wholes. The resulting aesthetic image clearly shows the character of the region through a contemporary vocabulary. The strong relationship with culture, myth, and history in Grupo de Diseño Urbano's projects reveals the firm's established interdisciplinary design groups that include archaeologists, botanists, historians, poets, engineers, and all the design professions.

Grupo de Diseño Urbano is internationally recognized for its innovative work in landscape architecture, architecture, and urban design. It has been engaged in a wide variety of projects including urban parks, museums and cultural centers, housing projects, and recreational and tourist developments.

William Thompson has written in *Landscape Architecture* magazine: "They see their trade as opportunities to uncover the hidden treasures of land and cultures. That revelation has taken the form of a major urban design project. True, Schjetnan and partners have designed private houses and gardens that are highly evocative of Mexican culture, such as his own house in Malinalco that blends village adobe with Modernist design sensibility. But his signature work consists of projects of truly Olmstedian scale and scope that call on his skills as building architect, landscape architect, and planner. The scale and power of their work have elevated the role of the landscape architect in Mexico. Schjetnan's projects are remarkable for the way they unite social concerns, aesthetics, and, increasingly, ecology–all by way of interpreting and celebrating Mexico's rich and diverse culture...."

Parque Tezozomoc
Mexico City, Mexico

Parque Tezozmoc is a 70-acre (28-hectare) public park in the District of Azcapotzalco, Mexico City. The park's topography and lake are a re-creation and narrative of the Valley of Mexico's lacustrine geography as it was in the fifteenth century.

▲
The topography of the park was executed with recycled dirt excavated from the construction of Mexico City's number six metro line. The water for the lake is recycled from a nearby water treatment plant and is used for irrigation of plants, flowers, and grass areas.

Parque Historico Culhuacan
Mexico City, Mexico

Parque Culhuacan is a one-hectare park in the District of Iztapalapa, Mexico City. The historic park is on an archaeological excavation of a pre-Hispanic port and is adjacent to a sixteenth-century former convent, which is now a popular cultural center.

The park is both symbolic and interpretative. It celebrates and introduces visitors and the local community to the area's history and myths.
▼

◄ Small outdoor rooms and plazas provide sites for open-air classes. The pavement's textures punctuate plazas and vistas, marking and delineating spaces.

▲
The living room opens directly to the patio and water mirror. The fireplace is used on cool nights. The patio forms a microcosm of all elements of nature: water, fire, stone, plants, earth, and sky.

Schjetnan House, Malinalco
Malinalco, Mexico

Schjetnan's weekend house is in Malinalco, a small town 66 miles (110 kilometers) southwest of Mexico City in a beautiful, lush, subtropical valley. Set in a preexisting orchard, the house is organized around a central patio.

▲
The bedroom entrances can be found in a long corridor.

Parque Ecologico Xochimilco
Mexico City, Mexico

The canal, lagoons, and agricultural island of Xochimilco are the last remnants of the lacustrine culture of the Valley of Mexico. Schjetnan's restoration work on the park includes a new lagoon, a flower market, and new *embarcaderos* or piers in an area of 690 acres (276 hectares).

▲
The entry plaza to the park is marked by a water tank, a symbol of ancient Archimedes' screws built to transport water over great distances in ancient aqueducts in Mexico.

Parque Ecologico Xochimilco
Mexico City, Mexico

In the entry plaza, a flower *paseo* or promenade with a continuous pergola of 440 yards (400 meters) invites visitors into the park. At the end, the *embarcadero* offers trips into the ancient canal and agricultural islands.

◄ A new *embarcadero*, with the traditional Trajinera flat-bottom boats, provides trips on the canals to the lagoons and *chinampas*, agricultural islands.

The market, with eighteen hundred flower stalls holding a wide variety of plants, is designed in a combination of pedestrian walks and plazas with separate streets. The overall image is a controlled metaphor of an agri-industrial landscape.

Grupo de Diseño Urbano
Fernando Montes de Oca no. 4
Colonia Condesa, México City
06140, México
phone | 52-5-553-1248
fax | 52-5-286-1013

CLIENTS

Gobierno del Estado de Aguascalientes, México

Gobierno del Estado de Chihuahua, México

Club de Golf Malinalco

Delegación de Azcapotzalco

Delegación Xochimilco

Instituto Nacional de Antropología e Historia, México

Instituto Nacional del Seguro Social, México

Secretaría de Educación Pública, Estado de México, México

◀ The water mirror in the round central court of the visitors center reflects the blue walls crowned with the symbolic Maguiey agave plants.

Terence G. Harkness

Terence G. Harkness' recent work explores the cultural and physical landscapes as sources for landscape design. By observing physical processes and sifting through local and regional cultural history, Harkness finds that a vocabulary of design emerges which is unique to each landscape. A wellspring of physical elements and patterns shapes his work as he strives to create places of strong visual presence and shared experience.

Harkness' design speculations are based on the idea that the common cultural-physical landscape often is a reflector of diverse, diffuse, and often ambiguous cultural expression. His landscape architecture seeks to order and create new places that are rooted in the common landscape and common experience. These places use and re-create the elements and experience rooted in the landscape of humans' personal and shared lives. With parts and organization that express social as well as physical patterns intrinsic to a particular time, people, and region, these built places are an evocation and abstraction of the world in which we live.

Garden Stories: A Suburban Garden

In Harkness' designs, the broad landscape establishes the order of the transformed place. His plan for a suburban garden in Illinois, for instance, reflects the directness of activity and the economy of rural places typical of the midwestern United States.

The youthful glacial landscape of east central Illinois has a distinctive pattern consisting of openness, carefully incised fields, a broad flat plane of property lines, overlapping roadways and railways, and a fine tracing of streams and rivers. Closely following the streams and rivers on the flat expanse of prairie are standing combs of woodlands, isolated groves, and remnant woodlots. Punctuating this horizontal scene are precisely constructed cubes, rectangles, and cylinders of homes, barns, storage bins, and machine sheds.

At this level of construction, one sees domestic green panels that define the farmyard and barn lot. The farmyard is the inhabited center of rural life. With their plain building materials and the attachment to the ground, the farm structures establish permanence even in this vast setting, where the economy of expression is softened only by a few specimen trees.

In Harkness' design for the suburban garden, his design vocabulary includes the flat, green plain; defined, incised edge; and asymmetrical building placement. The geometry confirms the orientation and order of farm and field. The edge containment of visual space is carefully managed, in keeping with the larger landscape. The house's essential orientation is outward, recalling a farm's active outward orientation to farm, field, and the changing seasons, sunlight, weather, and crops.

With this established order of ground plane and building arrangement, the garden also is linked to the larger context by three characteristic plant communities: shrub lands, woodlands, and remnant prairie strips. Remnant hedgerows and windbreaks, which survive in the larger landscape where farm machinery hasn't imposed its need for more space, become the visual frame for the garden. From the far distance, woodlands are combined with volunteer gray dogwoods, sassafras, sumac, and haws found along field edges. Bands of grassland and prairie forbs intermittently survive along railways and highways. These background woods, middle-ground volunteer successional shrub lands, and remnant prairie strips are drawn into the garden directly beyond the house lawn. These plant communities are telescoped into two abstracted bands, a tree/shrub border and a grassland border. Standing squarely in the open, as the buildings themselves do, a few large specimen trees cast shade and shadow across the garden lawn.

In the garden, gutters and downspouts gather rainwater from building roofs and direct the

water to splash-block/cisterns. The rain events pass directly in view from the drain-fountain into a traditional field of bulbs, daylilies, and hardy perennials. The flower garden is the "kept" garden, a traditional exclamation of seasonal flower beds for home and grounds.

That last refuge of the garden, the lawn and garden shelter, provide respite at day's end. Here Harkness transforms the rural corn crib into a constructed garden shelter of shade and pattern with a wooden screen of open slats. This open building has moveable sides that open and close, giving protection from the sun and wind as needed and permitting breezes to circulate during warm humid weather. The unattached building stands as a quiet, unadorned object. The suburban garden is about the subtle local landscape vividly transformed as a particular experience of place.

Krannert Swale Garden
Krannert Museum,
University of Illinois
Champaign, IL, USA

The proposed renovation of the south face of Krannert Museum re-creates an earlier landscape experience when the site was a geographically youthful expanse of imperfectly drained grasslands and isolated prairie groves in east central Illinois. The landscape now inhabited by a community and university originally was traversed by a flat, shallow prairie drainway that periodically flooded with spring and summer rains.

The landscape renovation for the museum is a distillation and abstraction of the character of the early prairie grassland and swales which periodically became bands of reflected water winding through the warped flat expanse of the region. In Harkness' design, this landscape of extremely subtle tipping and sloping, along with its intermittent ponding, has become an abstraction of landscape.

In the Krannert Garden, the swale is sliced lengthwise in half, and the wet centerline is retained by a white marble seat wall slowly following the curve of the drainway. Below the wall is a carved curving marble trench that floods with seasonal rainfall. When rainfall exceeds the open channel capacity, water temporarily flows over the surrounding lawn in a silvery flat sheet. At night, recessed lighting within the swale creates a ribbon of light which is brighter than the dusk sky and luminescent silver in the darker night sky.

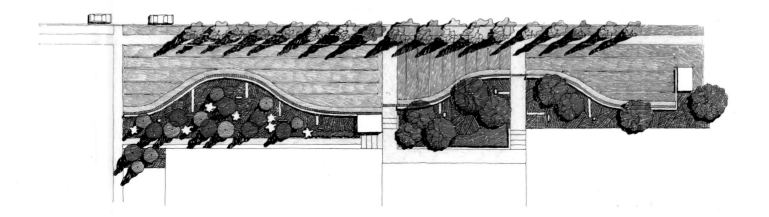

This wet half of the garden is about the essential quality of rainfall, runoff, and flooding. Its form captures the lingering release of the Midwestern thunderstorm. In addition, this part of the garden is designed to link to childhood memories, perhaps of playing in the temporary pooling of summer rain in low-lying areas of green lawn.

The other split half of the garden is the grassland and wooded grove on the lee side of the prairie swale. The grassland is protected from grass fires by its wet drainage course. The garden also incorporates the engraved patterns of farm fields against the distinctive remnant oak groves.

The Krannert Swale Garden is a smaller, more personal landscape place nesting in the larger campus setting. The garden is meant to tell landscape stories that are common to our past and are still active today.

Regional Airport:
A Common Landscape

The regional airport explores specific ways the cultural and physical landscape can be a source for the design of functional spaces that support everyday experiences. The design concept of the airport site is similar to the idea of an interpretive history garden–the distillation and comparison of several essential experiences and patterns of the larger landscape. The armature for the landscape design is shaped by the airport's fundamental organizing themes and the revelation of patterns of land ownership, agriculture, watercourses, woodlands, and prairie openness.

Two geometric forms are brought into intersection and juxtaposition in the airport design. The first, a cultural pattern of the larger landscape, is the square-mile grid typical of land in the Midwest. Second is the geometric pattern of a wind rose diagramming typical wind directions in this part of the country, a pattern clearly expressed in the layout of the airport and its runways.

Because of the need to manage wind and snow around the airport, vegetation as a wind-control element is a third element of the airport design structure. The hedgerows that traditionally have defined fields in the Midwest are important as wind and snow control devices.

By bringing together the major plant communities of the region in the design, Harkness incorporates a fourth element that further heightens the experience of east central Illinois. From the window of an aircraft or on the ground in a car, the airport landscape reveals ever-changing planted farmlands, prairie grasslands, and woodland groves. The disposition of these plant communities and the road alignments are such that the

viewer's attention is directed at or away from each planting type. With the roadway acting as an edge, the field, prairie, and woodland experiences all are linked together. In the design, the observer passes closely by each planting type, seeing the seasonal changes of prairies, forbs, and grasses as vividly as the cycles of the cultivated farm landscape are seen along any country road. Seasonal changes of the woodland grove, another prominent plant community of the region, are also readily apparent. With its black winter silhouette or arching green shade in summer, the grove is a powerful contrast to the flatness of the rural landscape.

A fifth aspect of the design organization relates to ways humans historically have come to terms with this landscape, specifically through the state-supported road system. After many of the state's new paved roads were completed, the Civic Improvement Associations of the 1920s promoted tree plantings along the highways. In this spirit,

trees line the road that leads to the terminal and links the open prairie planting on the east with the closed, wooded shelter belt of the north and west. Finally, the airport design is shaped by another historic precedent, the establishment of rural drainage districts with common ditches to remove excess water from the prairie. Rural drainways continue to be important elements of the local landscape. In the airport design, drainways are not for water removal but instead are presented as visible channels of water detention and conveyance. With design juxtaposition bringing the tree-lined drives and drainage channels into alignment, the channels serve as a linear, horizontal seasonal rain gauge, heightening the viewer's experience of water cycle and rainstorm events. Notched weirs express rainfall amounts by depth of overflow across the weir notches, extending and flattening the flood peaks by controlled detention and release. Seasonal and daily changes become immediately apparent.

This expression of the physical and the ephemeral elements of landscape links the design concept and plan. Whether arriving or departing by plane or car, travelers are confronted with these visible cultural and environmental benchmarks or gauging stations. This is what Harkness means when he says designers have the ability to tell the stories of landscape and culture in an abstracted, distilled way. To involve others in the creation of made places is a heightened way of sensing the past, the present, and perhaps a future. Thus Harkness' speculations are about designers' ability to splice, seam and draw together elements in a man-made place.

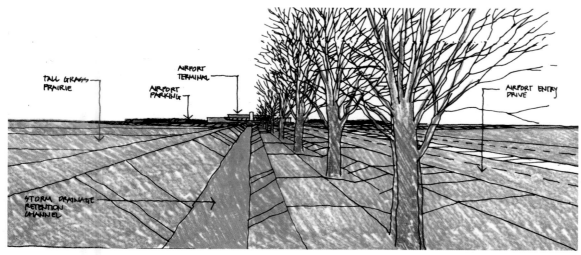

Terence G. Harkness
Landscape Architecture/Planning
1023 W. Charles Street
Champaign, IL 61821, USA
phone | 217-398-6308
fax | 217-244-4568

CLIENTS

East Central Illinois Regional Airport

Krannert Museum, University of Illinois

Hough Woodland Naylor Dance Limited

While Hough Woodland Naylor Dance Limited has long undertaken traditional urban design and development projects, it also is recognized for a broad range of work in urban ecology and regional landscape planning. The firm's underlying ethical philosophy stresses protecting and restoring natural settings by integrating environmental concerns with human use and activity. Of primary concern, therefore, are the intelligent application of ecological principles to the human landscape and finding design solutions that achieve multiple environmental and social benefits.

The essence of ecological design is constant transition, and the firm recognizes that the completed project is only the beginning, not the end, of a continuing evolutionary process. In an ecological sense, this is true of physical landscapes and restoration processes. It also is true of human communities and cities. Thus the firm regards its work as a continuum influenced by the people who use the landscape, as well as by evolving natural processes, economics, and changing values and objectives. In this sense, every project is new at any point in time, evolving from one state to the next.

Since its founding in 1963, Hough Woodland Naylor Dance Limited has focused on a variety of project types, including major parks and gardens, urban and civic design, university planning, urban ecological design and restoration, landscape management, housing and resorts, waterfronts, tourism, and institutional site development.

Ontario Place
Toronto, Ontario, Canada

A series of artificial islands, canals, and buildings suspended over the water in the city of Toronto. A major tourist attraction, Ontario Place offers opportunities for leisure and entertainment while celebrating Toronto's history and location on Lake Ontario.

The west island. The main pathway following a ▶
quiet interlinked canal system in a protected
oasis of trees and grass. This landscape offers
a marked contrast to the open, sunny, and often
windy environment of the lake side.

◀ The arrival area on the mainland overlooking
native perennials toward the building "pods"
housing exhibits. A covered walkway links the
mainland with the Ontario Place complex.

Casa Loma Gardens
Toronto, Ontario, Canada

The terrace at Casa Loma Gardens, site of
extensive plantings, sculpture displays, and
educational events. With their mix of classical
forms and romantic imagery, the gardens are
designed to reflect the formal splendor and
idiosyncrasies of the Castle, a landmark overlooking the city.

◀ A walk to the lower woodland gardens features
informal planting textures and brick paving to
provide a transition to the wooded area.

LaSalle Park Fish and Wildlife Habitat Restoration
Hamilton, Ontario, Canada

Coastal forces play a key role in the design of a carefully integrated program of fish enhancement structures and shoreline habitats. Through a series of restoration techniques, the newly armored shore is transformed into a natural shoreline condition.

Muck beaches and a shallow shoreline transition area respond to coastal forces and are oriented to attract and support specific species, such as pike, bass, and walleye. The beaches' shallow slopes also allow for inshore migration of amphibian species.
▼

▲
The grading of the beach landscape to its natural level reconnects the inshore wetland to the lake, while a raised boardwalk allows public access to the sensitive wetland without creating a barrier to wildlife.

"Discovery Routes" of the Near North

The plan created partnership implementation initiatives and established a new marketing strategy for the area, capitalizing on the many landscape assets which for so long have been unappreciated and taken for granted.

▲
The trail corridor management plans balance issues of intensity of recreational use, ecological sensitivity of the landscape, and maximizing opportunities for activities during all seasons.

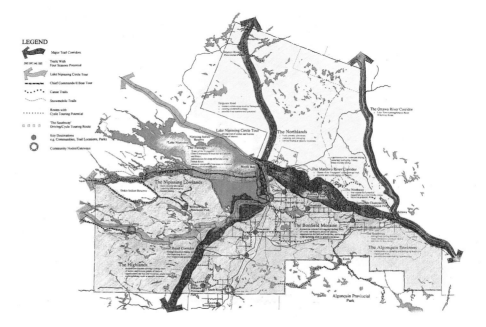

A trail system plan designed to attract new local ▶ and tourism markets by linking attractions, and natural and cultural features of the huge region of Ontario.

Bringing Back the Don
Toronto, Ontario, Canada

The healing of an urban river, spearheaded by the Task Force to Bring Back the Don, a group of Toronto citizens. This view looking north from the mouth of the Don River illustrates the problem: River channelization, expressways, railways, and utilities have degraded the river's lower reaches and destroyed habitat.

◄ On a field trip, members of the Bringing Back the Don Task Force survey the river's natural pools and riffles.

The beginning of implementation. A new area for ▶ accessing the bikeway that links two parts on either side of the river, providing the first bikeway access in some 5 miles (8 kilometers).

Upstream the Bloor Street Viaduct crosses a more
natural and peaceful place along the river.

Hough Woodland Naylor Dance Limited
961 The East Mall, Suite B
Etobicoke, Ontario M9B 6K1, Canada
phone | 416-620-6577
fax | 416-620-9546

CLIENTS

Action Committee

**Charlottetown Area Development
Corporation**

Garden Club of Toronto

**Hamilton Harbour Commissioners,
Hamilton Harbour Remedial**

Near North Trail Partnership

**Ontario Place Corporation,
Government of Ontario**

**Task Force to Bring Back the Don,
City of Toronto**

JMP Golf Design Group

JMP Golf Design Group is an internationally renowned golf course architectural firm with a reputation for creating award-winning courses with masterful landscape design. The essential philosophy at JMP centers on the belief that exceptional golf course design is truly an art form executed on a grand scale. For each project, JMP's designers attempt to successfully combine the classic traditions and principles of imaginative golf design with contemporary technology to create memorable, enduring golf courses.

All of the firm's principals are registered landscape architects possessing both an inherent and trained sense of the natural setting. They strive to ensure that every JMP project presents the player with a high degree of visual drama and beauty in concert with the golf course's surrounding environment.

Project types range from private country clubs and full-service resorts to semi-private facilities and public courses. The full scope of JMP's design services includes site evaluation, environmental assessment, conceptual master planning, detailed construction documentation, landscape design, construction supervision, and maintenance evaluation.

A U.S.-based firm, JMP has been involved in the design of more than two hundred championship golf courses throughout the world which have been constructed in a wide range of environmental settings. Underlying the creation of every new JMP golf course is a commitment to the centuries-old principle of strategic golf design, ensuring that each hole presents a challenging and enjoyable experience for golfers at all levels of ability.

Tomisato Golf Club
Tomisato, Chiba Prefecture, Japan

The seventh hole from tee to green. The rock outcropping and small pond that creates the hazard on this hole are actually JMP-designed features made of lightweight concrete.

Caledonian Golf Club
Chiba Prefecture, Japan

The fifth hole from the tees toward the green.
A beautiful par 3 that plays across a gently flowing stream and small lake. The landscape design
subtly blends with the natural setting.

▲
Same view of the fifth-hole tees (in bloom)
toward the green. The landscape treatment
becomes brilliantly spectacular in spring, when
azaleas, redbuds, dogwoods, and cherry trees are
in full bloom.

Gainey Ranch Golf Club
Scottsdale, AZ, USA

Aerial view of the ninth hole of the Arroyo Golf Course showing part of the five-star Hyatt Gainey Ranch Resort Hotel. The interplay of water and golf creates the visual centerpiece to this 500-acre (200-hectare) resort and residential development.

View from the completed ninth hole of the Lakes Course toward the clubhouse. The site was transformed by the use of landforms and the movement of water.

Rajpruek Club at Northpark
Bangkok, Thailand

View of the fourth hole. The site for this golf course presented JMP with a variety of technical challenges since the terrain was flat, treeless, and without satisfactory soil types. The completed colorful, rolling course makes a dramatic statement about the transformative power of landscape architecture.

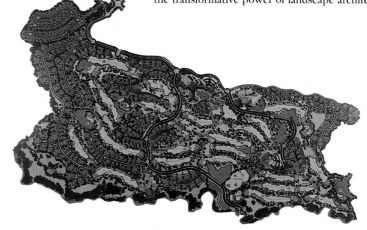

Bukit Pelangi Resort
(Rainbow Hills Resort)
Bogor, Java, Indonesia

View of the fourteenth hole from the tees, and golf routing and master plan. Built on hilly terrain surrounded by extinct volcanoes and tropical vegetation, the golfing experience at the twenty-seven-hole Bukit Pelangi Resort truly is unique.

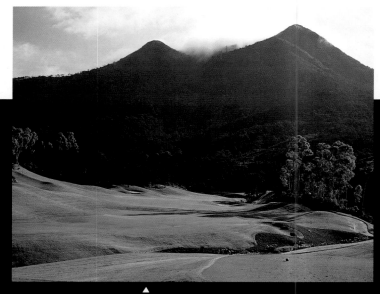

Long Island Golf and Country Club
Chang An, Guangdong Province, China

View of the green, waterfall, and stream on the fourth hole north. This entire feature was designed and created by JMP, illustrating the level of landscaping detail typical of the firm's golf courses.

▲
View from the tees of the fourth hole north. The famous Lotus Mountains of southern China act as a spectacular backdrop. The landforms of this hole depict JMP's bold shaping style.

The teeing area of the seventh hole north before construction and during initial clearing. This is a good example of the type of terrain in which championship golf holes may be created.
▼

View from the tees of the seventh hole north after construction. The completed hole shows how a difficult setting can be transformed into a beautiful golfing experience.
▼

CLIENTS

Active Realty and Development

Arimura Construction Company, Ltd.

Kajima Corporation

Land and Houses

Maddusalat Sdn. Berhad

Markland Properties

P.T. Light Instrumenindo

Reno/Sparks Convention Authority

Richland Development Company

Tokyo Green Company, Ltd.

JMP Golf Design Group
14651 Big Basin Way
Saratoga, CA 95070, USA
phone | 408-867-5600
fax | 408-867-9680
e-mail | http://www.jmpgolf.com

Carol R. Johnson Associates Inc.

One of the largest landscape architectural firms in the United States, Carol R. Johnson Associates creates landscape designs for both urban and natural environments. With an international clientele and long-standing relationships with many of the United States' leading architects and engineers, this firm is known for creatively integrating natural systems with built features.

Carol R. Johnson Associates' approach to design and problem-solving combines innovative technologies with environmentally sensitive design. The firm is adept at working with complex and challenging sites for which standard landscape design may not be appropriate or desirable.

The firm's work at Lechmere Canal and Park in Cambridge, Massachusetts, exemplifies its design capabilities. The central organizing feature of a neighborhood-wide revitalization, the park was coordinated to reclaim underused land and to allow the public access to a riverfront. Surrounded by both residential housing and office buildings, the canal edges are now an attractive promenade, and industrial shipping wharves have been replaced to allow public access. With a beautiful simplicity of scale, the design evokes the graceful architecture of the late nineteenth century.

Carol R. Johnson Associates' eight principals bring to their roles wide-ranging experience in the practice of landscape design. Their combined expertise includes park and recreation design; golf course planning; transportation projects; land reclamation; institutional design for universities, schools, and public housing; institutional and urban revitalization projects; and urban waterfront planning. Over the years, the firm's projects have been recognized by such organizations as the National Endowment for the Arts, the American Society of Landscape Architects, and the U.S. Department of Transportation.

Lechmere Canal Park
Cambridge, MA, USA

Working closely with agencies of the city of Cambridge and a neighborhood task force, the firm developed the park concept based on the historic importance of the Lechmere area as a nineteenth-century industrial center. The park reclaims underused land and transforms a once-deteriorated area into a functionally diverse and active urban center.

John Fitzgerald Kennedy Park
Cambridge, MA, USA

A series of gateways, steel picket fences, and plantings create soft green spaces for informal recreation. The focus of the park is a fountain memorial to President Kennedy, located on axis with a pedestrian link to Harvard Square. The fountain features smooth, transparent sheets of water falling over polished granite walls.

State House
Boston, MA, USA

A comprehensive site restoration program included a new plaza and garden on top of an underground parking garage.

Wellesley College Sports Center
Wellesley, MA, USA

The reconstruction of Wellesley College's outdoor athletic facilities is part of a larger landscape design program for enhancing the varied topography of the campus and solving problems created by new buildings, new pedestrian patterns, and the increased dominance of the automobile on campus.

Wildflower Meadow, Wellesley College
Wellesley, MA, USA

The master plan for Wellesley's campus includes strategies for preserving endangered vegetation and enriching the existing greenery.

Headquarters, Ocean Spray
Cranberries, Inc.
Lakeville/Middleboro, MA, USA

Carol R. Johnson Associates prepared site analysis and feasibility studies for seven different land parcels for this new headquarters. The firm then directed the efforts of the site consultant team and supervised construction of all site elements. In addition, CRJA prepared an environmental impact report.

Carol R. Johnson Associates Inc.
1100 Massachusetts Avenue
Cambridge, MA 02138, USA
phone | 617-868-6115
fax | 617-864-7890

CLIENTS

Boston Housing Authority

City of Cambridge, MA

City of Boston Metropolitan District Commission

Connecticut Department of Transportation

Duke University

Harvard University

Massachusetts Highway Department

Massachusetts Port Authority

National Park Service, USA

New York State Department of Transportation

Ocean Spray Cranberries, Inc.

City of Taipei, Taiwan

Wellesley College

Jones & Jones

Portland International Airport Parkway
Portland, OR, USA

The approach to Portland International Airport celebrates air travel. Leaving the freeway, curving between windbreaks of local stone, the traveler passes through wing-like chevrons of endemic Lombardy poplars and native incense cedars. From the air, the traveler gets a broader sense of the sculptural arrangements of trees and stone.

Twenty-seven years ago Jones & Jones was created to bring the perspective and expertise of several professional disciplines to bear on the development of the built environment. The senior partners deliberately created an innovative integration of architecture and landscape architecture as the foundation for this diversified practice.

At Jones & Jones, architects specialize in making the essentials of the landscape the major terms of reference, and landscape architects work with buildings as an integral part of the landscape. Each influences and challenges the other to inhabit the natural and urban landscape with built forms that resonate with an intrinsic sense of place.

Jones & Jones works cooperatively with clients to promote innovative design solutions. The firm's pioneering work with zoological and botanical gardens, aquariums, cultural institutions, regional and recreational planning, urban parks and greenways, and scenic conservation planning demonstrates a commitment to cultural and natural resources.

The firm is renowned for bringing to fruition distinctive projects throughout North America, Mexico, and many Asian countries. They are recognized internationally for their commitment to excellence and design achievement.

The eye is led outward by the angles and increasing ▶
distance between chevrons, to the Columbia River
and Mount Hood, enduring emblems of Portland's
regional sense of place.

Occidental Square Park
Seattle, WA, USA

Jones & Jones prepared a master plan, designed, and led construction of two plazas in Seattle's historic Pioneer Square district. A former parking lot and little-used street became a vibrant urban gathering space, framed by London Planetrees and centered around a pergola and two totem poles.

◀ The streetscape of Occidental Square complements the historic character of the Pioneer Square district. London Planetrees shade a cobbled square, and a popular cafe spills out along one side, inviting pedestrian activity throughout the day.

Mercer Slough Nature Park
Bellevue, WA, USA

Formerly a marsh along Lake Washington, Mercer Slough was used for log storage at the turn of the century. The area is slowly returning to its former vitality due to Jones & Jones' master plan and design of low-impact wetland trails, interpretive centers, and a blueberry farm and retail outlet.

Part of the city's open space program, Mercer Slough is a source of life for a diversity of plants and animals. The park also is a haven for urbanites seeking quiet and contemplative exploration. ▶

Thai Elephant Forest, Woodland Park Zoo
Seattle, WA, USA

Jones & Jones pioneered the design of zoological exhibits such as the Elephant Forest. The firm authored the principle of landscape immersion, in which visitors share the animal's domain, and view them with few or no visible barriers in close simulations of each species' natural setting.

Sleeping Lady Retreat and Conference Center
Leavenworth, WA, USA

Harriet Bullitt commissioned Jones & Jones to help create a mountain retreat for nonprofit and conservation groups, a place that would inspire cooperation and renewal. This unprecedented project, recipient of several awards for energy efficiency and eco-tourism, demonstrates development that is site sensitive, environmentally sound, and rooted in a regional aesthetic.

◄ The design of Sleeping Lady minimized the removal of trees, and the few that were sacrificed were milled on site and used for construction. Much of the construction waste was mulched and used in an organic garden whose produce is used for the retreat's gourmet dining.

Gene Coulon Memorial Beach Park
Renton, WA, USA

Gene Coulon Park is a very popular urban beach. The building–a restaurant, boathouse, picnic shelters, and maintenance facilities – recall turn-of-the-century lakeside pavilions. Walkways and trails wind through natural settings, including a revitalized salmon stream.

◄ Situated south of Seattle, Gene Coulon Park is a narrow greenbelt between a rail line and Lake Washington. One-third of the park encompasses intense recreational activity–boating, fishing, swimming, tennis, and group picnicking. The rest of the park offers quieter, more isolated outdoor experiences.

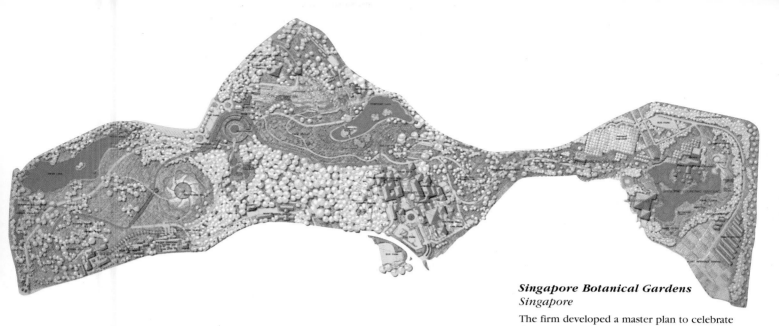

Singapore Botanical Gardens
Singapore

The firm developed a master plan to celebrate the gardens' 130th anniversary and guide development for the next twenty years. The plan gives priority to the gardens' renewed role as a valued botanical, horticultural, and recreational resource in equatorial Asia.

▲
Jones & Jones' master plan provides a blueprint for the basic physical layout of the gardens. The team designed the Orchid Gardens for the launching of the new twenty-year plan. Orchids are an important crop and symbol for Singapore.

Jones & Jones
105 South Main Street
Seattle, WA 98109, USA
phone | 206-624-5702
fax | 206-624-5923

CLIENTS

Arizona-Sonora Desert Museum

Bellevue Parks & Community Services Department

Harriet Bullitt

Busch Gardens, Busch Entertainment Corporation

Mountains to Sound Greenway Trust

Portland Airport Authority

City of Renton Parks Department

City of Seattle Department of Parks & Recreation

Singapore National Parks Board

John Tillman Lyle, FASLA

John Tillman Lyle's work as an educator, researcher, and designer focuses on the ongoing processes of regeneration in the landscape and their integration in human life and culture. Through design, he believes, humans participate in nature's larger, dynamic patterns of evolutionary renewal. If we participate with wisdom, creative thought, and sensitivity, we nurture the order of nature and the richness of life. We also help sustain both nature and human culture in a world where the future of both is uncertain.

To accomplish this, Lyle believes humans need to see, comprehend, and design the landscape in both very large and very small terms–the encompassing patterns of entire geographic regions down to the rocks and trees that form particular places. Lyle's work encompasses various perspectives, ranging from watershed planning and management, to regional planning and urban design, to institutional and recreational development, to the design of gardens.

Much of Lyle's effort has been devoted to the highly collaborative 606 Studio that he and Professor Jeffrey Olson developed at the Department of Landscape Architecture at California State Polytechnic University in Pomona. In the Studio, advanced graduate students work under the direction of faculty teams to carry out large-scale ecological planning projects for public agencies. The projects focus on complex environmental and resource issues, usually with far-reaching political and social implications.

In his own practice of landscape architecture, Lyle primarily focuses on the site and project scales. He does not maintain an organization but works on a direct personal basis with clients and teams of professionals suited to the issues and locale of each project.

A highly acclaimed educator and the author of two books on ecological design, Lyle has received or shared ten national awards from the American Society of Landscape Architects for his work in design, planning, and communication; and in 1996 received the ASLA Medal, the society's highest award for professional achievement.

Lyle Garden
Sierra Madre, CA, USA

This small garden is designed to reflect and join the small personal world of the owners with the massive and precipitous San Gabriel Mountains that loom nearby.

The garden's forms reflect the jagged shapes of the mountains and the hard rectilinear forms of the city, which meet and merge in ways that suggest the washes at the base of the mountains where rainwater seeps into the ground to replenish the groundwater basin. ▶

Appalachian Ministries Regional Educational Center
Berea, KY, USA

The master plan for the center's 80-acre (32-hectare) site includes examples of farmland revitalization, wetlands habitat enhancement, prairie restoration, sustainable forestry, water treatment, and other ecological processes suitable for the renewal of Appalachia.

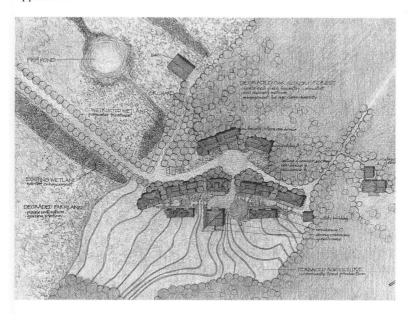

Model: Ming Shieh-Hung, Yutaro Terada, Sara Trifiro, and Sabrina Faucher

▲
The village is set against the edge of an oak and hickory forest, with the center's buildings clustered around a central gathering space and amphitheater. The structures are passively solar heated and draw upon the architectural themes of rural Appalachia.

Center for Regenerative Studies,
California State Polytechnic University
Pomona, CA, USA

The Center for Regenerative Studies, where students learn about regenerative systems for basic life support by incorporating them into their daily lives.

▼

Project initiation, conceptual and schematic design: John Tillman Lyle, FASLA; and the Cal Poly interdisciplinary design team
Design development, construction documents: The Peridian Group, Landscape Architects; and Dougherty and Dougherty, Architects

▲

Native walnut trees (foreground) provide habitat for nesting hawks, owls, and other wildlife, which continue to live in close proximity with humans.

Community agriculture and aquaculture, where ▶
residents grow much of their own food, are
integral parts of the center's living environment.

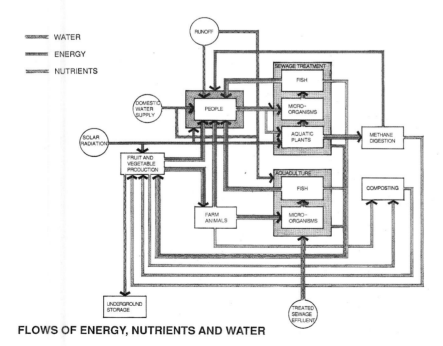

WATER
ENERGY
NUTRIENTS

FLOWS OF ENERGY, NUTRIENTS AND WATER

▲
This diagram, which was a key tool for design of the university-
based community, analyzes flows of energy and materials.
It illustrates the ways in which the center functions as a human
ecosystem, using energy from the sun and continuously cycling
and re-assimilating materials through biological processes.

School of Theology at Claremont
Claremont, CA, USA

The School of Theology has committed to reshape its campus landscape according to regenerative principles, thus demonstrating a theologically based policy of caring for the earth. At the core of the landscape master plan is a small demonstration complex based on the principles of the Center for Regenerative Studies.

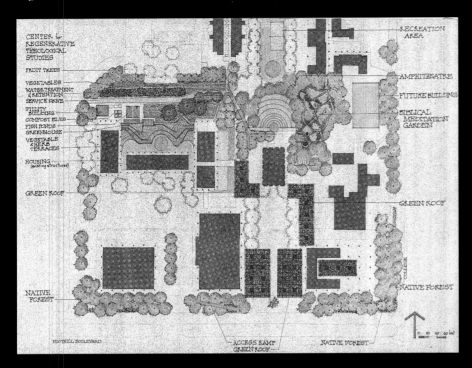

The initial project in the plan is a biblical meditation garden, designed as a network of winding pathways that converge on a pond and waterfall representing renewal of life. Diverging paths offer places to pause for thought. ▶

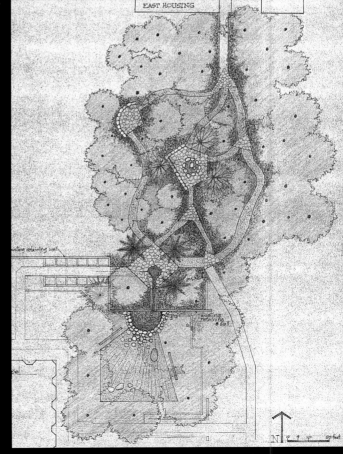

▲
The garden uses recycled materials: broken concrete for paving, wood chips from nearby trees for mulch, composted manure for soil enrichment. Rocks were found on the site or nearby. Runoff water is retained on-site.

John Tillman Lyle, FASLA
580 N. Hermosa
Sierra Madre, CA 91024, USA
phone | 909-869-2684
fax | 909-869-4460

CLIENTS

Appalachian Ministries Educational Resource Center

Browning-Ferris Industries

California State Polytechnic University

**Ente Flumendosa
(Water Management Agency)**

City of Lompoc, California

Oberlin College

School of Theology at Claremont

Southern California Edison Company

Regional Government of Trentino

Steve Martino & Associates

The profession of landscape architecture sustains growing division over the concerns of ecological design, artful design, and socially responsible design. Steve Martino & Associates' body of work shows how these concerns can be addressed successfully in unison to create sustainable landscapes of great beauty, cultural context, social consciousness, and ecological richness.

Steve Martino, FASLA, ceaselessly promotes the virtues of a climate-adapted environment and timeless design. He is known for his pioneering work with native plant material and the development of a desert-derived aesthetic. Martino's work consistently has addressed the difficult conflicts of contemporary expectations in an environment whose foundation is a sensitive desert landscape.

Martino seeks to develop environments that express a sense of identity, reality, and wholeness with the site-places that respect and intensify the unique feeling of the region. Each design strives to incorporate the better aspects of humans' relation to history and the landscape, adding meaning to a project which often transcends the client's original expectations. Martino often finds inspiration in the substantive current issues facing society and nature.

Project experience ranges from urban development to private gardens to remote large-scale communities. Martino's work includes desert plant species experimentation and commercialization, habitat restoration, and the creation of public landscapes that impart a strong sense of unique regional identity.

Steve Martino & Associates' innovative work has earned more than seventy-five local, regional, and national design awards, including six National American Society of Landscape Architecture Design Awards. In a fall of 1992 article on biodiversity, the *Amicus Journal* affirmed the success of his projects: "Landscape architect Steve Martino has created some of the most beautiful gardens ever produced by an American designer."

Arid Zone Trees
Queen Creek, AZ, USA

Formerly a cotton field, this farm specializes in growing desert trees for the southwestern United States. Martino's work has included creating a showcase entrance to the site, developing botanical gardens, creating seminar and plaza areas, and experimenting with re-vegetation techniques to restore the farmland back to a desert landscape.

Greenberg Residence
Paradise Valley, AZ, USA

A desert landscape relates this contemporary house to its environment in a neighborhood where Mediterranean-style landscapes have altered the native habitat.

Cholla Street Residence
Phoenix, AZ, USA

The remodel of a thirty-year-old desert hillside house included replacing all paving with native crushed stone, removing non-native trees and plants, and restoring the desert landscape. The yellow color on the wall is the dominant hue of the flowers on the hillside above.

Ullman Terrace, The Desert Botanical Gardens
Phoenix, AZ, USA

Ullman Terrace, a former paved parking lot, was transformed into an exhibit space, outdoor cafe and dining area, and setting for small performances and private functions. The terrace adds thirty new trees to the gardens and serves as a model for desert-inspired public environments.

Acacia Park Office Building
El Paso, TX, USA

The building face and courtyard walls are of native stone, a local traditional material for fences that had not been used in area buildings since the late thirties. The courtyard is influenced by historical forms and connects the two ground floors that are set 10 feet (3 meters) apart vertically.

Hawkinson Residence
Phoenix, AZ, USA

The side yard garden of a small urban lot celebrates the desert and cultural influences of the Southwest. A fountain wall focuses the space as well as the waters' sound back to the house. The water channel aligns with the summer sunrise and leads back to secret rooms.

De Bartolo Residence
Paradise Valley, AZ, USA

The landscape development, except for the courtyard, is a restoration and enhancement of the desert environment. The courtyard acts as an outdoor living room. The freestanding walls echo the house structure, with a window in the retaining wall allowing a view from the pool to the south.

The New Times Building
Phoenix, AZ, USA

When an abandoned historic school building was restored as a newspaper office, an outdoor courtyard garden with desert plants was created for employees. A fountain masks street noise while providing a focus for the space. The fountainheads are Arizona reptiles, created by sculptor Allan Weaver.

Steve Martino & Associates
3336 N. 32nd Street, Suite 110
Phoenix, AZ 85018-6241, USA
phone | 602-957-6150
fax | 602-224-5288
e-mail | smariz@aol.com

CLIENTS

Boulders Resort Clubhouse

The Desert Botanical Garden

El Paso Electrical Co.

Four Seasons Resort, Scottsdale

University of Nevada at Las Vegas

NFL Cardinals Training Facility

City of Phoenix

The Phoenix Zoo

City of Scottsdale

Thomas McBroom Associates Ltd.

Thomas McBroom has emerged as one of North America's finest golf course architects, with a succession of award-winning courses from coast to coast. At the heart of McBroom's philosophy is the profound conviction that no two golf courses are alike, and that each course should be inspired by the land upon which it is built. Each course the firm designs represents a collection of eighteen distinct vignettes, where every golf hole is a new game, every time.

Established in 1978, Thomas McBroom Associates has designed or constructed more than one hundred golf courses and golf course communities. McBroom's courses consistently rank among the finest and most beautiful in the country, and are noted for their outstanding playing strategies, distinctiveness, and memorability. Every course is crafted with an unprecedented attention to detail, scrupulous environmental consideration, and an extraordinary personal vision, which are all key to the creation of a great golf course.

Beacon Hall
Aurora, Ontario, Canada

The distinctive plantation pines framing the second green and third fairway add verticality to a beautiful site characterized by topographic variety. Beacon Hall was the first of two successful collaborations with U.S. golf course designer Robert Cupp.

Ottawa Hunt and Golf Club
Ottawa, Ontario, Canada

Originally laid out as an eighteen-hole course by the great Willie Park after World War I, the twenty-seven-hole Ottawa Hunt was completely redesigned by McBroom and rebuilt in the early 1990s. The Hunt hosted the 1994 LPGA du Maurier Classic.

▲
Two majestic white pines frame the second south hole and landing area, and the multilevel green is protected by deep bunkers.

Monterra Golf Course
Blue Mountain Resort, Collingwood, Ontario, Canada

This routing of this classic 6,500-yard (5,850-meter) par 72 resort course takes advantage of the natural features of the terrain. The unusual razorback mounds define the seventeenth hole fairway and echo the forms of the low mountains that surround the course.

The green on this short hole is well guarded by mounds and bunkers. The coffin in the lone maple (lower right) was a later addition by the director of golf, a sly reference to the coffin bunker at Scotland's Royal and Ancient St. Andrews.

The Links at Crowbush Cove
Morell, Prince Edward Island, Canada

Named the Best New Course in Canada by *Golf Digest* in 1994, the 6,900-yard (6,200-meter) par 72 Crowbush Cove is a unique blend of traditional golf course design and modern construction and environmental preservation techniques. Extraordinary lengths were taken at this seaside course to protect the sweeping dunes and natural saltwater ponds.

At the beautiful but difficult sixth hole, the tee ▶ shot is played over a tranquil pond and marsh running along the front and left of the green, which is guarded by deep bunkers and dramatic mounds.

One of the most dramatic finishing holes in golf, ▶ the elevated eighteenth tee offers exciting views to the clubhouse and a green guarded by heaving mounds and bunkers.

Le Géant
Mont Tremblant, Quebec, Canada

Opened in 1995 and runner-up as *Golf Digest*'s best new course in Canada, the championship-length 6,900-yard (6,200-meter) Le Géant winds around the base of Quebec's most popular ski resort through heavily glaciated terrain cloaked in hardwoods. Hole #10 Par 3, stacked bunkers of high contrast sand set against a granite wall, call for a precise tee shot.

The seventeenth hole offers an exciting risk-reward strategy with a deep ravine cutting across the fairway directly in front of the green. This golf hole is typical of a McBroom design in that it seems to lie effortlessly upon the land.

▼

Heron Point Golf Links
Ancaster, Ontario, Canada

Opened in 1992, the 6,800-yard (6,120-meter)
par 72 Heron Point is the home of the Canadian
Masters Tournament. Characterized by a liberal
use of water throughout the course, Heron Point
has three distinct topographies: hardwood forest,
meadow, and marsh.

Thomas McBroom Associates Ltd.
120 Carlton Street, Suite 305
Toronto, Ontario, M5A 2K1, Canada
phone | 416-967-9329

CLIENTS

Canadian Pacific Hotels and Resorts

CanLan Developments Inc.

ClubLink Corporation

Genstar Developments

Intrawest

Goverment of New Brunswick

Goverment of Prince Edward Island

City of Vancouver

Moorhead Associates & Forrec Ltd.

West Edmonton Mall
Edmonton, Alberta, Canada

At 4 million square feet (360,000 square meters), West Edmonton Mall is the largest shopping mall in the world. It also represents the first real attempt to integrate leisure, retail, and hospitality under one roof. The 4-acre (16-hectare) indoor World Waterpark is landscaped with tropical plants to create a South Pacific ambience.

Client: Triple Five Corporation

Landscape architecture involves a way of thinking about the environment, both natural and developed, that can be brought to many different tasks. Moorhead Associates, in conjunction with Forrec Ltd., has applied the ideals of landscape architecture to an extremely broad range of design exercises, from the conventional to the outlandish. The Moorhead Associates portfolio includes public gardens and parks, civic squares, residential and commercial landscaping, and master planning. However, the main focus of attention, in conjunction with Forrec Ltd., is the planning, design, construction, and management of leisure and entertainment facilities. In all of Moorhead Associates' endeavors, one goal remains paramount: that the work and the product be accessible, enjoyable, and represent the highest quality.

The Trinity Square project in Toronto is an example of a conventional project that succeeds because of its unconventional approach. By offering a variety of environmental experiences, Trinity Square welcomes and entertains a large and diverse group of people every day. There is an attraction for every inclination.

In the realm of unconventional projects, Moorhead Associates has a number of achievements, including the world's largest indoor water park (West Edmonton Mall), Canada's first major theme park (Canada's Wonderland), and one of Asia's largest indoor theme parks (Central City Bangna, Thailand). These and other projects are distinguished by their careful development, from feasibility through planning to detailed design and construction. Consideration of the comfort and entertainment of potential users is top priority.

Moorhead and Forrec employ about sixty staff in offices in Toronto and Singapore, comprising landscape architects (the largest group), architects, technologists, and specialists in such fields as graphic, interior, theater, and urban design.

Moorhead Associates is an affiliate company of Forrec Ltd., of which Steven Moorhead is chairman. Some of the work included here has been executed by other partnership configurations, with Moorhead as a principal partner.

Trinity Square
Toronto, Ontario, Canada

In the midst of one of Toronto's busiest commercial and retail areas, just steps from Toronto's City Hall and adjoining the Eaton Centre and the headquarters of Bell Canada, Trinity Square is one of the most heavily traveled urban squares in Toronto's downtown core. The trinity of squares provides the framework for the creation of a series of multifunctional spaces with arcaded walks, a grass lawn, plaza areas, fountains, and sculpture.

Client: The Corporation of the City of Toronto and the Cadillac Fairview Corporation Ltd.

Universal Studios Florida
Orlando, FL, USA

Universal Studios Florida was designed as the world's most spectacular movie studio theme park as well as a working production facility. The key areas are New York (right), San Francisco, Amityville, Expo, and the Front Lot.

Client: An MCA/Rank Organization joint venture

In addition to master planning, design development, and area development, Moorhead Associates also designed and executed construction drawings for the theme facades. Pictured: New York back alley.
▼

Dazzleland
Niagara Falls, Ontario, Canada

In the Clifton Hills tourist area of Ontario's Niagara Falls, Dazzleland is a family entertainment center that includes an eighteen-hole miniature golf course with contoured fairways, family games, and a video arcade.

Client: HOCO Ltd.

Canada's Wonderland
Maple, Ontario, Canada

Canada's first large-scale amusement park has several attraction areas, each with its own fantasy theme, surrounding a 150-foot (45-meter) constructed mountain. In his book *White Knuckle Ride*, Mark Wyatt called Canada's Wonderland, "One of the most beautifully land-scaped theme parks in the world." The planning, site development, and detailed site design of this 350-acre (140-hectare) attraction presented a unique challenge in complexity and scope.

Client: Canada's Wonderland Ltd.

Aqua Resort Panamá 2000
Panamá

A 2,000-acre (800-hectare) destination resort adjacent to the Panama Canal, Aqua Resort Panamá 2000 offers a unique underwater environment that includes a "lost" city, themed attractions, scientific facilities, and an underwater hotel.

Client: Promoción y Desarrollo Turístico, S.A.

Dreamland
Cairo, Egypt

Dreamland is the centerpiece of a proposed 5,000-acre (2,000-hectare) mixed-use development in Sixth of October City, Cairo, Egypt, within sight of the pyramids at Giza.

Client: Dr. Ahmed Bahgat Fatouh/Dreamland

Fiesta Texas
San Antonio, TX, USA

Fiesta Texas is a 200-acre (80-hectare) entertainment theme park spectacularly situated at the bottom of a quarry enclosed by 80-foot- (24-meter-) high cliffs. The spill-waters increase the site's natural drama.

Client: Opryland Real Estate USA/USAA

Mediterranean Village
Gateshead, U.K.

In an 80,000-square foot (7,200-square meters) secondary artery of Metrocentre Mall, landscape elements and a Mediterranean village theme were introduced to revive activity. The traffic area was converted to a meandering street with new storefronts and four restaurants with outdoor-style patios.

Client: The Church Commissioners, Metro Shopping Center, Gateshead, U.K.

Moorhead Associates & Forrec Ltd.
211 Laird Drive
Toronto, Ontario M4G 3W8, Canada
phone | 416-696-8863
fax | 416-696-8866

CLIENTS

Government of Abu Dhabi

Canada's Wonderland Ltd.

Canberra, National Capital Development Commission

Dreamland, Egypt

Harvard University

Hyundai Sungwoo Group

MCA/Rank Organization

Province of Ontario

Opryland Real Estate USA

Ottawa, National Capital Commission

Shaw Brothers, Hong Kong

Siam Radio/TV

South Malaysia Industries

Suzhou New District

Municipality of Metropolitan Toronto

Triple Five Corporation

Universal Studios Florida

Villages of Lady Lake, Florida

Walt Disney Imagineering

Morgan Wheelock Inc.

Arrow International Corporate Headquarters
Reading, PA, USA

The challenge for this project was to successfully site a new suburban corporate headquarters building with parking on 125 acres (50 hectares) of idyllic rolling farmland. Using pear trees, a wildflower meadow, a lawn, and existing hedgerows, the design sensitively preserves the open feeling of the existing landscape.

Morgan Wheelock's designs are based on a deep respect for nature and a belief that human experience is enriched by diverse and intimate contact with the natural world. This attitude is expressed through close integration of built forms with the planted forms in which they are placed; careful composition of the varied spaces of a landscape into an ordered and sensible pattern; and the use of a broad planting palette to emphasize the passage of time throughout the seasons of the year. Strong spatial design allows forms to be understood quickly on a large scale, while the detailed composition of garden elements and plantings sustain interest at a more intimate level and over a longer period of time.

The firm's design approach enhances and preserves qualities that are unique to an individual site. The qualities inherent in the land often are expressed in the finished landscape design, together with a recognition of the local natural forces that will influence a design as it matures.

Morgan Wheelock Incorporated has offices in Somerville, Massachusetts, and Palm Beach, Florida. Since 1978 the firm's work has encompassed a broad spectrum of projects including corporate and institutional campuses, arboretums and botanical gardens, resort and residential communities, equestrian farms, and residential estates.

United States Armed Forces Memorial Garden
Caen, France

The United States Armed Forces Memorial Garden commemorates sacrifices made by American military personnel during the D-day invasion and subsequent World War II battles. It was constructed on the grounds of a museum in Caen, France, which was the site of bunkers used by the German command.

Becton Dickinson World Headquarters
Franklin, NJ, USA

This complex of office and research buildings
was given form through a master plan creating a
central grand garden and courtyard. The buildings become the walls to the garden and forest
site, which dominates the corporate campus.

Private Farm
Richmond, MA, USA

The master plan for this 200-acre (80-hectare) farm included the siting of a new home plus landscape design for a hunter/jumper horse facility. The driveway and gardens emphasize distant views to the Berkshires.

Private Residence
Cape Elizabeth, ME, USA

Morgan Wheelock's master plan for this 260-acre (104-hectare) site has been implemented over a period of fifteen years. It includes woodland gardens, a pond, an entrance drive and service areas, a swimming pool and cabana, and cutting gardens.

Private Residence
Fishers Island, NY, USA

A reflecting pool and broad stone terrace are
central to the design of this waterfront site.
Gardens off the side of the house are framed
by native vegetation.

Private Residence
Palm Beach, FL, USA

This Tuscan-style oceanfront house is organized
around a formally inspired entrance court
flanked by a croquet court and framed by high
hedges. Broad steps in the lawn provide a base
for the architecture.

Private Residence
Cambridge, MA, USA

A historic Shingle Style house designed by H.H. Richardson forms the backdrop to this garden, which features planting, fencing, and arbors stylistically linked to the period architecture.

Lanes End Farm
Versailles, KY, USA

Planning for a new 1,600-acre (640-hectare) thoroughbred horse farm for broodmares and yearlings involved the siting of barns, roadways, and fences, in addition to landscape design.

Morgan Wheelock Inc.
362 Summer Street
Somerville, MA 02144, USA
phone | 617-776-9300
fax | 617-776-9333

235 Peruvian Avenue
Palm Beach, FL 33480, USA
phone | 561-655-9006
fax | 561-655-9007

CLIENTS

Arrow International

Battle of Normandy Foundation

Becton Dickinson and Co.

Dallas Arboretum and Botanical Garden

Harvard Business School

Landscape Architecture: The Heart of the Matter

s the work in this book suggests, the practice of landscape architecture today is about as diverse and complex as the landscape itself. Indeed, since the term *landscape architect* was first used in 1858, the struggle to define the profession has been continuous. The effort has intensified in modern times in response to radical changes in the American landscape since the 1930s, and, more recently, to a broadening set of environmental landscape problems. Through it all and despite our sometimes passionately expressed differences, the profession continues to share a unifying, fundamental concern for trying to create the kind of space that can orient people to the land in their time.

Before the 1850s (just prior to the American Civil War), there was little need for a profession of landscape architecture in North America. With some notable exceptions in a few designed cities and estates, the pre–Civil War, North American landscape of wilderness and evolving agriculture allowed most people more than enough opportunity to make direct and personal connections to the land. By the 1850s, however, it was becoming clear to Frederick Law Olmsted and Calvert Vaux, among others, that a profession of "landscape architects" was needed to provide public and private landscape space in response to increasing urbanization and industrialization.

From this birth of the profession of landscape architecture until the mid-1930s, landscape architects chiefly participated in the creation of magnificent urban parks such as Olmsted and Vaux's Central Park in New York, as well as country places and European-style villas for wealthy industrialists. In response to the increasing loss of people's direct connections to the land, they also attempted to make contemporary landscape spaces where these connections could be felt and

"Boys in a Pasture,"
1874, Winslow Homer. The Hayden Collection.

Courtesy, Museum of Fine Arts Boston, Massachusetts.

Though modern in some ways, classical elements persist in Beatrix Farrand's Dunbarton Oaks.

Post-relativity, complex, modern space exhibited in this James Rose garden.

understood. Landscape architects became involved in city and town planning and in the creation and design of state and national parks, not to mention parkways.

It should be noted, however, that as late as the mid-1930s, the U.S. was still primarily an agricultural society, with over fifty percent of the population involved directly or indirectly in agricultural pursuits. Much of the American landscape still consisted of well-kept farms, orchards, and vineyards, which afforded most Americans a wholesome, direct, and personal connection to the land.

The modern practice of landscape architecture began with the arrival of three rebellious students at Harvard's Graduate School of Design in 1936. Dan Kiley, James Rose, and Garrett Eckbo rejected the antiquated Beaux-Arts axial system of design taught at Harvard (and elsewhere) because, as Rose wrote in *Pencil Points*, "such a system did not consider change, particularly the change in world point of view, that came with the Industrial Revolution and the Theory of Relativity." Based upon a keen sense of their rapidly-changing times, their incisive writings and built works ushered the profession—sometimes kicking and screaming—into the modern era. The quickly disappearing landscape of farms helped clarify the modern landscape architecture profession's task: How could landscape architects create the kind of space that would orient people to the land in a mechanized, industrialized, urbanized society?

After World War II, the vision of these pioneering modern landscape architects became irrefutable as the population exploded, and the urban and suburban landscape virtually replaced the agricultural one.

*While involved in solitary or group
activities, people also engage the land at
Durfee Gardens, a contemporary park.*

Now most Americans' experience of the landscape changed from that direct and personal connection achieved through the agricultural garden and landscape to a more symbolic relationship in cities and rapidly growing suburbs. A modern profession of landscape architecture was desperately needed to create space for the orientation of people to the land in designs of suburban backyards and communities, shopping centers, recreational parks, corporate headquarters, college campuses, and urban centers. Modern landscape architects also began to engage in planning whole regions and to work internationally. While attempting to solve new types of problems in a time of explosive change after World War II, the profession was constantly redefining itself even as it defined the expanding American and international landscape.

Modern landscape space took on a very distinct look from that of the previous period. New and recycled materials such as concrete block, fiberglass, and old railroad ties replaced Italian marble and other imported and expensive materials in gardens and landscapes. Previously based upon classical formulas or romantic nostalgia, the basic composition and geometry of landscape space itself changed. The older design principles were replaced by a new enthusiasm for a kind of design where form and space would organically evolve directly from the unique characteristics of a given site and the contemporary needs of modern people. Referring to the "old methods" of designing according to preconceived principles, James Rose once quipped, "Cripes, even if you could find a site just like the Villa d'Este [a famous sixteenth-century Italian Villa], where are you going to find Mr. d'Este?"

Existing site features, such as these rock outcroppings in a James Rose garden, are often the inspiration for design in modern landscapes.

The proliferation of landscape project types and professional practices has continued and undoubtedly will continue to grow. By executing projects of all scales and types, the profession is reconsidering the relationship between art and ecology, and personal expression and social function, planning and improvisation, and design and sustainability. It is rethinking its relationship to architecture and to the fine arts, and forging even deeper ties with a broader range of consulting specialists.

At the end of the twentieth century, in our current information age, with global economic, social, and ecological imperatives, landscape architecture appears poised for yet another redefinition of the profession. In the process of broadening the practice of landscape architecture to deal with the increasingly complex problems of life on earth, it is still our ability to make spaces where people may again connect directly with the land in our times that defines this profession and is at the heart of what it means to be a landscape architect.

Dean Cardasis, Landscape Architect and
Associate Professor, University of Massachusetts, Amherst

Murase Associates, Inc.

Japanese-American Historical Plaza
Portland, OR, USA

A memorial to acknowledge the internment of more than 110,000 Japanese-American citizens during World War II. The story of confinement is depicted in bronze relief and in poetry engraved on the standing stones. This master plan illustrates the overall design and site context of the plaza.

Established in 1982, Murase Associates maintains offices in Portland, Oregon, and Seattle, Washington. Robert Murase, founding principal, gradually has added associates to his practice who complement his own strengths and interests, thus enabling the firm to offer a wide range of services. The firm's core disciplines are landscape architecture and urban planning. Projects range widely in scale, from large regional concepts to plazas, squares, and gardens. The firm has developed master plans and design guidelines for large urban and waterfront projects; designs for urban plazas and streetscapes; and plans for housing and new town facilities.

Murase's design solutions speak in a language that is about our inner nature and that seeks to reveal our personal experience. In their simplicity, his designs are suggestive rather than explicit, where the participant is asked to derive a personal interpretation of place. Murase is drawn to the challenge of expressing large concepts in his work, alluding to regional and local physical and visual design connections and seeking to understand the largeness of our being by the smallest details. He builds by choosing a limited palette of materials and then forging highly refined and selective details.

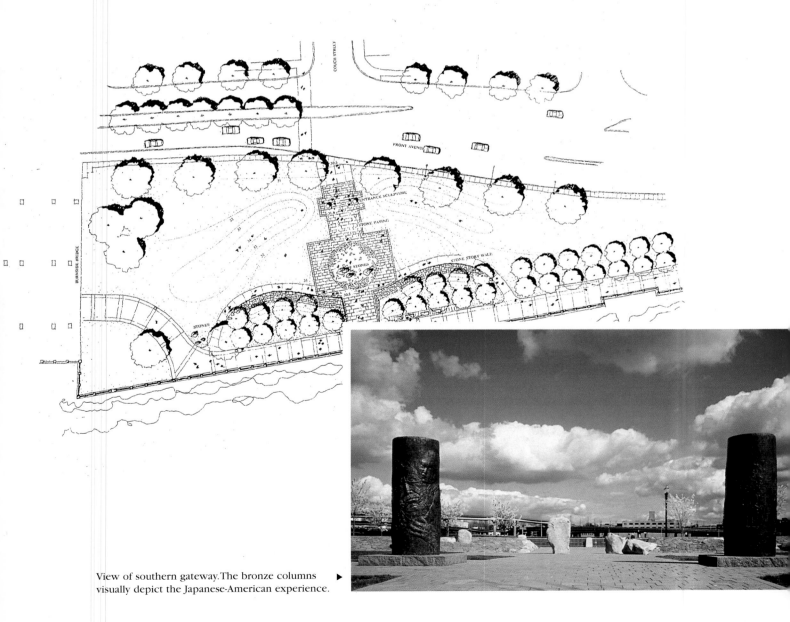

View of southern gateway. The bronze columns ▶
visually depict the Japanese-American experience.

The mood and resonance of the plaza are
transformed with the changing of the seasons.
The stones are visually connected with each
other, a relationship that seems to change as
visitors move between them.
▼

▲
Within the central plaza, three of the largest
granite stones move outward from the break
in the basalt story-wall defining the order of
the center.

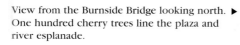

View from the Burnside Bridge looking north. ▶
One hundred cherry trees line the plaza and
river esplanade.

War and change,
My native land
Once so hard to leave,
Is behind me now
forever.

Glancing up
At red-tinged mountains
My heart is softened.
A day in deep autumn.

▲
Talking stones in the Japanese-American
Historical Plaza.

Collins Circle, West Side Light Rail, Tri-Met
Portland, OR, USA

A traffic circle on the edge of inner-city Portland, Collins Circle was redesigned by the firm in concert with the development of the Westside Light Rail Transit project to serve not only as another place for cars, but as a gateway to the city. The large, tilted stone sculpture that was installed at the site symbolizes the rebirth of the city neighborhood, and draws parallels with the burial mounds and megaliths of prehistory, the stone gardens of Japan, and the volcanic activity that has shaped the Pacific Northwest. Seen from a car or a train under changing light, the stone circle, punctuated with standing stones and three gnarled Sumac trees, is an ever-changing place of wonder and meditation.

◀ A sumac tree and stone emerge out of the cracks in the field of basalt.

Pier 69 Atrium
Seattle, WA, USA

Located along the waterfront of Puget Sound, the restored Pier 69 structure is the Port of Seattle's headquarters. As this view from behind the granite tower illustrates, Murase's intent for the project was to articulate forms and their edges in simple and clear compositions.

The sweeping curved granite entry bench expresses an open, welcoming gesture and modulates the atrium's axis.

A stone basin covered by a film ▶
of water reflects the serenity
the space provides.

Private Residence
Woodside, CA, USA

Renovation plans for this 5-acre
(2-hectare) estate included
development of garden spaces,
terraces, meadows, and a swimming pool and pool terrace.
The plant material selected for
the garden are native to the
region. Shown: Lush planting
and the terrace beyond.

Murase Associates, Inc.
1300 N.W. Northrup
Portland, OR 97209, USA
phone | 503-242-1477
fax | 503-295-0942

320 Terry Avenue N.
Seattle, WA 98109, USA
phone | 206-622-9458
fax | 206-622-6835

▲
The vibrant plant material provides color and
softens the edges of the hardscape.

CLIENTS

Brown and Caldwell

CH2M Hill

HOK

Kallmann, McKinnell and Wood

Microsoft Corp.

National Park Service, USA

Nike, Inc.

Parsons Brinkerhoff Quade & Douglas, Inc.

The NBBJ Group

Port of Seattle

Tri-Met Oregon

University of Washington

ZGF Partnership

City of New York Parks & Recreation

The City of New York Parks & Recreation's landscape architecture division is one of the largest landscape design offices in the United States. With forty in-house landscape architects, Parks & Recreation is responsible for approximately $50 million of projects annually as New York City upgrades its public recreation facilities, builds and restores new parks, and enhances the ecology in natural areas.

The range of work requires skill in many areas, including historic preservation, design of playgrounds that are accessible to the disabled, wetland restoration, and design of community recreation complexes. Parks & Recreation's landscape architects come from Haiti, Poland, Holland, Japan, Taiwan, China, Canada, and many different regions of the United States. In addition to receiving training in landscape architecture from various universities, a large proportion of the staff holds advanced degrees in such fields as architecture, historic preservation, city planning, urban design, biology, and fine arts. Staff diversity enables the landscape architecture group to respond to numerous project types, working with various types of communities, political pressures, and environmental contexts.

Parks & Recreation is responsible for rebuilding existing parks, creating new facilities on recently acquired land, reprogramming outdated spaces for contemporary use, and improving the ecology of New York City by improving water quality and increasing permeable green space and wildlife habitat. The landscape architecture group has developed the design and planning methods now used to combine recreation design, environmental remediation, and restoration/management of historic landscapes.

The landscape architecture division's design philosophy is to respond to the needs of local communities, which is expressed through encouragement of community participation and the lobbying of elected officials. Features of many parks are being redesigned to suit current needs and laws. Preserving New York's cultural history also is vitally important. The Parks and Recreation department has provided one hundred years of continuous design work on the same pieces of land, so many New York parks share a stylistic heritage that today's professionals are dedicated to preserving.

Cobble Hill Park
Brooklyn, NY, USA

A bird's-eye view of Cobble Hill Park shows its geometric form as well as the contrasting colors of the brick, granite, and green landscape.

Designer: Ralph Borkowski, RLA

Columbus Park
(Brooklyn Borough Hall)
Brooklyn, NY, USA

The reconstructed downtown civic area restores a triangular park setting originally surrounding the city hall which existed in the mid-1800s. The redesigned park uses a nineteenth-century vocabulary developed through researching historical photographs. The creation of a mall visually connects Borough Hall to the Manhattan Bridge.

Designer: George Vellonakis with Wim deRonde, ASLA; Emmanuel Thingue, RLA

Manhattan Beach (Pat Parlato) Playground
Brooklyn, NY, USA

This 1-acre (.4-hectare) active playground within Manhattan Beach Park includes basketball courts, handball courts, a water spray, interactive sundial, and three play units. The largest unit is built around a 36-foot (11-meter) long concrete pirate ship.

Designers: Steve DesNoyer, RLA; Jackson Wandres, RLA

City of New York Parks & Recreation 159

McNair Park
Brooklyn, NY, USA

This $1.2 million project adjacent to the Brooklyn Museum incorporates such durable materials as bluestone and granite. The park is home to a contemporary sculpture by artist Ogundipe Fayomi memorializing the late Dr. Ronald McNair.

Designer: Marcha Johnson, ASLA

Twin Islands Salt Marsh Reconstruction
Bronx, NY, USA

In 1995 this $90,000 project reestablished a one-acre inter-tidal marsh. By excavating a naturalistic new tidal channel and planting native grasses and shrubs, a fragment previously isolated has been rejoined to Pelham Bay Park's marine ecosystem.

Sara Delano Roosevelt Park
New York, NY, USA

In response to years of neglect and deterioration at the park, the schematic study focuses on revitalization. Major objectives are to incorporate the inherited original design, improve physical conditions and environmental quality, and support positive park uses.

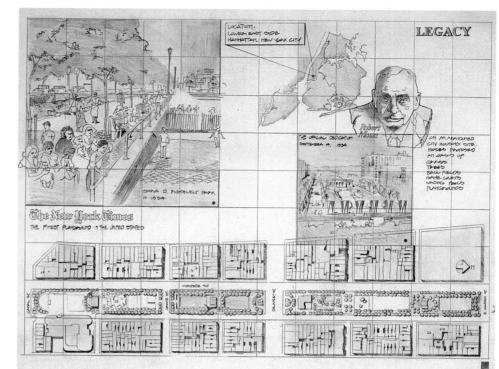

Designer: Jason Yu, RLA

Powell's Cove Park
College Point, NY, USA

The new 12-acre (4.8-hectare) Powell's Cove Park is on a former construction dump site from which more than 2,500 tons of debris will be removed. Targeted for completion in 1997, the project includes wetlands restoration and construction of pathways and overlooks to create a naturalized shoreline park at the mouth of the East River.

Designer: Angela W. Fowler, RLA, with Marcha Johnson, ASLA

City of New York Parks & Recreation   161

Queens County Farm Museum
Little Neck, NY, USA

The Queens County Farm Museum, a 7-acre (2.8-hectare) living history museum, is a designated New York City landmark site associated with the Jacob Adriance house. The museum is the last vestige of Queens' three-hundred-year history of agriculture. The most recent project provided utilities to the museum, restored a greenhouse, and constructed a roadway.

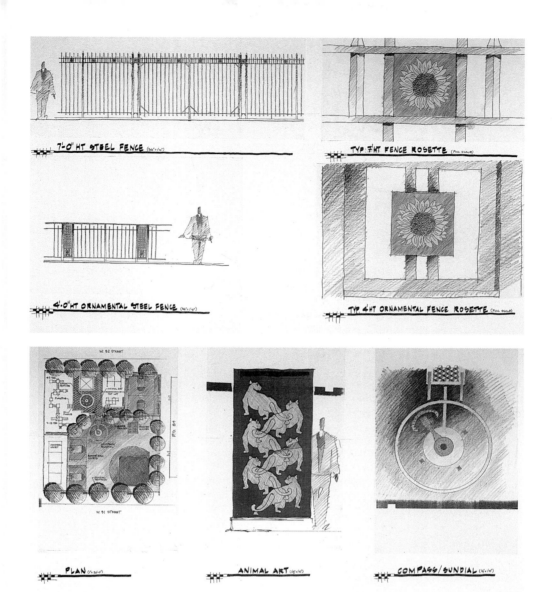

Designer: Emmanuel Thingue, RLA

Sol Bloom Playground
New York, NY, USA

The colorful pavement, artwork, and vibrant
sunflower motif form strong whimsical patterns,
which, combined with a climbing apparatus and
analemma-style sundial, form a playful environment.

City of New York Parks & Recreation
Olmsted Center
Flushing Meadows-Corona Park
Flushing, NY 11368, USA
phone | 718-760-6613
fax | 718-760-6666

Cornelia Hahn Oberlander

Cornelia Hahn Oberlander Landscape Architects, a small office founded in 1953, is dedicated to "greening" urban areas through innovative techniques based on the tried-and-true as well as on research of new technologies. By investigating alternative solutions as part of the planning and design process, the firm thrives on discovering creative solutions to complex problems. Working as a member of a team with architects, the firm seeks to meld the built form into the landscape. This philosophy is expressed in projects such as the three-block urban park of the Provincial Government Complex, the Vancouver Public Library, C.K. Choi Institute of Asian Research, and the Northwest Territories Legislative Building. All projects show strong, simple concepts and a vision dedicated to preserving the natural environment.

Over the years Cornelia Hahn Oberlander Landscape Architects has developed a wide variety of expertise; in children's playgrounds, beginning with the innovative creative playground at Expo '67 in Montreal; roof gardens and hanging planters, as in the award-winning landscape for the Canadian Chancery in Washington, D.C.; native plant communities, such as the firm's project at the Taiga Garden at National Gallery of Canada in Ottawa, Ontario; and with environmental planning and design, as at the C.K. Choi Institute of Asian Research. Much of this expertise also has been incorporated into landscape architecture site design projects for urban plazas, large civic projects, and private residences.

Social responsibility and environmental sensitivity guide all Cornelia Hahn Oberlander Landscape Architects projects. The resulting plans and designs are responsive to both the site and the users, and are healthy spaces that bring pleasure throughout the seasons.

Robson Square, Provincial Government Complex
Vancouver, British Columbia, Canada

Architect: Arthur Erickson Architects
Landscape Architects: Arthur Erickson Architects; Cornelia Hahn Oberlander; Raoul Robillard

Robson Square is an oasis in the center of the city. Waterfalls and water walls provide sound and motion.

▲

The three-block Provincial Government Complex
landscape shows that the art and skill of the
architect, engineer, and landscape architect are
mutually supportive. Together, the project team
created a unique urban environment that
imports nature into the city.

◀ The use of a lightweight growing medium allowed total integration of plant material on roofs and in planter boxes, thereby providing both large and intimate spaces for people living and working downtown. Robson Square has become a landmark in the city of Vancouver and a visitor destination.

◀ This linear park in the heart of downtown Vancouver provides a wide variety of landscape experiences through sunshine and shadow. Large gathering areas filter out into green fingers of semiprivate walkways and quiet resting places.

Streets bordering the Provincial Government Complex are planted with a double row of Acer rubrum Red Sunset. The canopy of the maples extends the experience of the urban park to the curbside throughout the seasons. ▶

Northwest Territories
Legislative Building
Yellowknife, Northwest Territories, Canada

Architects: Ferguson Simek, Clark Pin Matthews,
Matsuzaki/Wright Architects

The severe climate of the Northwest Territories'
capital city offered a complete range of challenges. New techniques for obtaining plant
material had to be researched.

Archietcts: Ferguson Simek, Clark Pin Matthews, Matsuzaki/Wright Architects

▲
The capital site landscape celebrates life in the
north, with its light and darkness, regional plants,
and seasonal beauty. Shown here: fall color on roses.

▲
The inherent beauty of the landscape was preserved and restored. Mats of peat bog with plant
material were carefully lifted from construction
areas and replanted.

C.K. Choi Institute of Asian Research, University of British Columbia
Vancouver, British Columbia, Canada

Architects: Matsuzaki/Wright Architects

Along the street a columnar form of Gingko biloba (maidenhair tree) was selected to absorb pollutants and allow maximum light into the building.

A greywater trench for water purification runs along the front of the building. The trench, lined with recycled PVC and filled with gravel, is a subsurface biological marsh, planted with reeds, sedges, and iris. The greywater is purified by natural processes and gradually released into a subsurface irrigation system.

▼

▲

The existing coniferous forest with trees more than 100 feet (30 meters) high and an undergrowth of salal, ferns, and huckleberries. Development was designed to preserve the natural ecosystem and to retain and extend an arboreal sense so that the building relates to the existing forest.

Library Square
Vancouver, British Columbia, Canada

Architects: Moshe Safdie Associates Ltd., Downs Archambault and Partners

Vancouver's new public library incorporates state-of-the-art technology to plant large caliper Liriodendron tulipifera street trees around Library Square. Planted in a continuous trench to promote linear root growth, the trees are in a growing medium that supports them while conforming to city engineering standards for compaction density.

▲
Cascading roses and white flowering dogwoods grow in planter boxes at the children's daycare center, where sunflowers are part of the summertime experience.

Cornelia Hahn Oberlander
1372 Acadia Road, Vancouver
British Columbia V6T 1P6, Canada
phone | 604-224-3967
fax | 604-224-7347

CLIENTS

Government of British Columbia

C. K. Choi Institute of Asian Research, University of British Columbia

Government of Northwest Territories

City of Vancouver

Olin Partnership

Committed to landscape architecture as a celebration of place, Olin Partnership believes in recognizing both the social and natural processes that shape a site. With design expressive of the genius loci–the spirit of the place–the firm has created landscapes that succeed as social spaces and as environmental systems. By synthesizing the best of art and science, Olin Partnership seeks to transform natural and man-made elements into expressions of social purpose, reconciling the character of the place with its contemporary adaptations.

The firm takes a long-term view of design, believing that strong, clear schemes supported by innovative detailing and fine, lasting materials are essential in melding social needs and physical resources. By blending functional accommodation, symbolic meaning, and aesthetic richness, the firm strives to design timeless human environments. Olin Partnership sees landscape architecture as a practical art that serves people, and it is committed to work that is biologically sound, socially just, and spiritually rewarding. The firm's approach synthesizes an economy of means and a generosity of spirit and accommodation. Olin Partnership's projects vary in appearance but not in substance or process. While each place in the world is particular and deserves a unique design solution, a constant in all of the firm's work is that it is intended for people who have recurring, timeless needs.

Vila Olimpica
Barcelona, Spain

Vila Olimpica is a private mixed-use development built in conjunction with the 1992 Barcelona Summer Olympic Games. Development of the 6-acre (2.4 hectare) site, including office, hotel, residential, and retail spaces, was part of Barcelona's efforts to institute a comprehensive redevelopment of its infrastructure and open-space system through the reclamation of abandoned and obsolete industrial sites adjacent to the city's waterfront.

The design creates a suite of outdoor rooms inspired by the culture and climate of Catalonia. The site is structured on the metaphor of a river valley flowing through the local agricultural landscape. Vibrant flower and shrub borders were inspired by the organic forms of the Spanish artist Miró and the patterns found in the early cubist work of Picasso and Braque.

▲
View from the rooftop planting structure to the garden terrace and herb parterre of the Hotel Arts at Vila Olimpica.

◀ The water feature at the entry and taxi drop-off area of the Hotel Arts at Vila Olimpica, directly beneath the rooftop planting structure.

Pershing Square
Los Angeles, CA, USA

Seen as key to the revitalization of downtown Los Angeles by both the public and private sectors of the city, Pershing Square became the focus of a major site analysis and reconstruction that addressed physical and social problems. A victim of the automobile age, this once verdant nineteenth-century park was excavated in the 1950s to build a three-level underground garage. A replacement park never transcended the isolation created when all sides of the space were severed from city street life by the garage's access ramps.

The design team reconnected the park to its neighborhood by redesigning the underground garage ramps to create space for new perimeter sidewalks and entries.

Pershing Square's entrances are now identifiable gateways, each with unique elements: a 125-foot (38-meter) campanile, a cafe, a transit station, and kiosks.

Once a single open space, the redesigned park is divided into two distinct squares differentiated by a grade change. The lower square contains a large basin fed by an aqueduct that mimics tidal fluctuations of the sea, filling and draining at regular intervals. Bosques of trees with benches surround the basin and provide shade. The upper square consists of an amphitheater and stage.

▲
Central axis through Pershing Square.

The tidal fountain with stone paving. ▶

Design: Olin Partnership; Legorreta Arquitectos

Bishopsgate
London, England

The Bishopsgate project is a prominent commercial/urban development in London's financial district. Adjacent to the Liverpool Street rail station and the Broadgate development, Bishopsgate creates a series of interconnected yet distinct exterior public spaces which reflect the rich historic context of the site. Significant landscape elements include a simply planted public square with a central raised lawn panel and a bosque of horse chestnut trees, as well as a fountain, kiosks, artwork, and a handsome stone amphitheater for events and performances. The Bishopsgate roadway is a major regional bus stop and was transformed into a large public room with new stone pavements, obelisks, railings, and stone benches for commuters.

▲
The central lawn panel at Exchange Square at Bishopsgate. Liverpool Street rail station is to the left.

◀ Exchange Square at Bishopsgate. Train shed is to the right.

Canary Wharf
London, England

As part of an international multidisciplinary team, Olin Partnership participated in the urban planning and site design for this mixed-use development on the River Thames at Canary Wharf, London. The development revitalized 71 acres (28.4 hectares) at the site of the West India Maritime Shipping Facilities docks. More than 10,000,000 square feet (900,000 square meters) of office accommodations designed specifically for the expansion of the financial services sector have been set within a strongly articulated public realm.

Urban squares, courtyards, boulevards, and esplanades are located over occupied space, which required the development of innovative construction and planting technologies to create the appearance of established landscapes using semi-mature plant materials.

▲
Outer ring of London Planetrees at West Ferry Circus, Canary Wharf, overlooking the River Thames. Large caliper trees were installed in innovative tree pits to create an instant mature landscape.

▲
Park in the inner ring of West Ferry Circus. The entire park is built on structure.

In front of the center, tilted planting beds and plinths planted with native grasses and flowers.

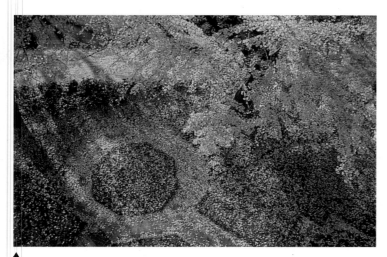

Autumn foliage on top of the tracery of the foundation of the building that originally occupied the site. These "ruins" are incorporated into the design of the facility.

Wexner Center for the Visual Arts, Ohio State University
Columbus, OH, USA

Olin Partnership's design for the Wexner Center, a new visual arts facility on the Ohio State University campus, integrates two existing buildings and the spaces surrounding them. The concept was inspired by combining two incongruent geometries: the city of Columbus street grid and the campus grid. The dynamics of a 12.25-degree shift between the grids were explored in both building and landscape, as well as in plan and section.

Major landscape elements include a pedestrian entryway into the campus, a bosque of trees which acts as a propylaeum for the central campus green, and a tilted amphitheater. Set within the organizing matrix are a series of raised and tilted plant beds enclosed by large sandstone plinths, which have become a signature of the center's integration of landscape and structure. Planted with a mixture of ornamental grasses and small flowering trees evoking the prairie landscape, the plinths establish a visual tension along the routes of entry and passage. Another prominent feature is an arrangement of brick walks, parapets, and seating walls that trace the outline of an armory building that once stood on the site. A piece of this tracery forms a garden richly planted with trees, shrubs, and perennials.

Battery Park City Esplanade
New York, NY, USA

Once a landfill, the site of Battery Park City was devoid of natural features such as topography, vegetation, and microclimatic diversity. Now Battery Park City, a 92-acre (37-hectare) residential and commercial development in lower Manhattan, encompasses an extensive public open-space system including a 1.25-mile-long (2-kilometer-long) riverside esplanade, several miles of streets, and many parks and squares. A vocabulary of pavements and site furnishings characteristic of New York City's public realm was incorporated into the design guidelines. The materials create a backdrop appropriate for public events and art displays.

▲
Waterside esplanade with the Statue of Liberty visible in the distance.

Waterside esplanade at Battery Park City.
▼

CLIENTS

Bryant Park Restoration Corporation

Denver Regional Transportation District

New York State Urban Development Corporation

Ohio State University

Olympia & York

Pershing Square Properties Owners Association

Rosehaugh Stanhope Developments

Travelstead Group and Skidmore Owings & Merrill

Olin Partnership
421 Chestnut Street
Philadelphia, PA 19106, USA
phone | 215-440-0030
fax | 215-440-0041

ROMA Design Group

Third Street Promenade
Santa Monica, CA, USA

With streets, plazas, and other gathering places as the principal stages for interaction, ROMA's design created a complex layering of uses and spaces that works together to make Third Street Promenade a seven-day-a-week success. The design included 30-foot-(9-meter) wide sidewalks to encourage pedestrian use and outdoor café seating. Banners, topiary dinosaurs, kiosks, trees, streetlights, and public art, as well as the variety of uses and activities, break the three 600-foot-(180-meter) long blocks into friendly, enticing centers of activity.

ROMA Design Group is a nationally recognized urban design and development planning firm with more than thirty years of experience in the United States and worldwide. It has helped shape the growth of dozens of cities, including San Francisco and San Diego, California; Seattle, Washington; and Portland, Oregon. The firm also has completed important projects in a variety of other states, including Florida, Texas, Colorado, Alaska, and Hawaii. Recent international projects include the Coal Harbour mixed-use development in Vancouver, Canada; a mixed-use complex in downtown Kuala Lumpur, Malaysia; the downtown plan for Manila, the Philippines; and Viaduct Harbour in Auckland, New Zealand.

ROMA's work in urban design primarily focuses on three major areas: designing lively public places, redeveloping urban in-fill sites such as former industrial districts and railroad yards, and creating attractive towns and identifiable regions. The firm builds on the distinctive qualities of each site, responding to community values and the existing natural and cultural environments to create a strong identity and sense of place.

ROMA helps communities accommodate their need for growth and change without damaging historic buildings and neighborhoods or threatening surrounding natural resources. When designing public places, the firm seeks to create an attractive pedestrian realm and a vibrant mix of activities to revitalize long-deteriorated streets and districts, create a greater sense of community, and encourage interaction between different social and economic groups. This approach can be seen in the firm's successful work in California cities, including San Francisco's downtown waterfront, the town center of Suisun City, downtown Santa Cruz, and the Third Street Promenade in Santa Monica.

While incorporating the most advanced and innovative approaches to environmental and urban design, ROMA's new towns and regional plans balance conservation and development; restore landmark buildings; strengthen historic neighborhoods; preserve and/or restore large amounts of open space; and create attractive, clearly structured public places. ROMA's plans establish a clear and exciting vision of a city's future.

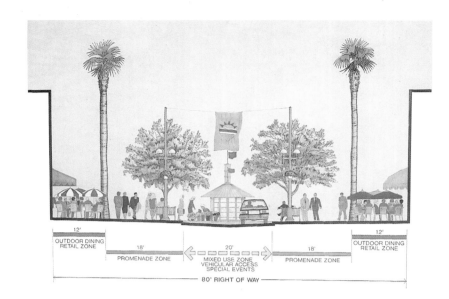

Redevelopment Plan
Suisun City, CA, USA

Since the early 1990s Suisun City has completed
more than half a dozen redevelopment projects,
attracting new residents and businesses to Old
Town and boosting municipal revenues. The new
Town Plaza overlooking the recently dredged
Suisun Channel is a vibrant community focal
point. A waterfront promenade, which runs past
a new 300-berth marina and along now-sparkling
Suisun Channel, offers the city's pedestrians their
first waterfront access in fifty years.

Embarcadero Waterfront
San Francisco, CA, USA

When the earthquake-damaged Embarcadero Freeway was demolished in 1991, San Francisco gained an opportunity to reclaim and revitalize its long-isolated and neglected central Embarcadero waterfront in front of the landmark Ferry Building and adjacent to the downtown business district.

Equally important, the city was able to carry out an integrated revitalization program for the entire waterfront, linking the northern and southern ends that had been separated from each other by the freeway's route along the central Embarcadero. The privately and publicly funded projects that are being carried out under the provisions of ROMA's Northeast Waterfront Plan include housing, mixed-use development, parks and open space, a new surface roadway for automobiles, two new trolley lines, and a 7-mile-long (11-kilometer-long) waterfront promenade overlooking San Francisco Bay. These projects are the nation's most significant waterfront redevelopment program since Battery Park City in lower Manhattan, New York.

ROMA has designed many significant projects along the San Francisco waterfront, such as the master plan for the South Beach neighborhood, which includes eighteen hundred apartments and condominiums, restaurants and cafés, neighborhood shops, and open space. ROMA designed the new Downtown Ferry Terminal behind the Ferry Building, as well as the nearby Pier 7, a fishing and recreational pier extending 845 feet (254 meters) into San Francisco Bay. Just offshore, ROMA prepared a reuse study for Treasure Island, site of the 1939–1940 Golden Gate International Exposition and a former United States Navy base.

ROMA helped prepare the reuse study for the rundown Ferry Building that dates to 1896, including the historic restoration of its facade and interior, seismic upgrades, and the addition of various retail and entertainment uses. The firm also designed the new Ferry Building Plaza which, according to the *San Francisco Chronicle*, will "become a premier public space, a combined park, promenade, and festive meeting place that would be unique in the world."

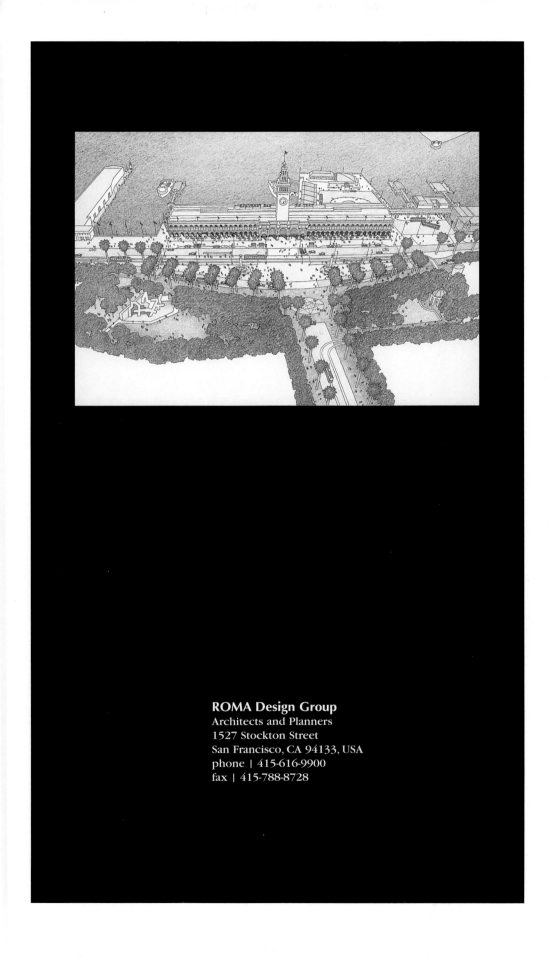

ROMA Design Group
Architects and Planners
1527 Stockton Street
San Francisco, CA 94133, USA
phone | 415-616-9900
fax | 415-788-8728

Department of Public Works
City and County of San Francisco, California

The Landscape Architecture Section for the City and County of San Francisco consists of a core of ten landscape architectural staff members. The section is part of the Bureau of Engineering, Department of Public Works, which otherwise comprises civil, mechanical, hydraulic, structural, and electrical engineers.

The Landscape Architecture Section provides services to agencies and departments responsible for the development, maintenance, and renovation of the city's rights of way, parks, squares, open spaces, and ancillary landscape areas. Clients include the Recreation and Park Department, Department of Public Works, Port of San Francisco, San Francisco International Airport, Public Utilities Commission, Municipal Railway, and San Francisco Redevelopment Agency.

Virtually all of the work performed by the Landscape Architecture Section occurs within the city's 49-square-mile (127-square-kilo-meter) area. What San Francisco lacks in size it more than makes up for in cultural and social diversity, rich history, and complex environmental conditions. Spirit of place varies greatly from one area to another, even within the city's distinctive districts.

The work of the landscape architectural staff reflects a planning and design process that incorporates the needs of the client agency while also fulfilling the desires of the community. As is typical for public works projects, the section's projects are designed to endure, both physically and as expressions of the people's aesthetic sensibility.

Designers of public landscapes in San Francisco at the close of the twentieth century also must be cognizant of social and political constraints: low maintenance budgets, vandalism, graffiti, homelessness, and fear of violent crime. Within this challenging context, the city's landscape architects attempt to design projects that are not only useful and durable, but also projects that often inspire San Franciscans and their visitors to reverie.

Shakespeare Garden,
Golden Gate Park
San Francisco, CA, USA

The 1991 renovation of the Elizabethan-style Shakespeare Garden focuses on formal symmetry, from the wrought iron entry gates to the central brick walkway flanked by crabapple trees. New walkways and seating areas with carved stone benches invite use for quiet contemplation or intimate parties and celebrations. Bronze plaques focusing on Shakespeare's love of flora enhance this literary setting in Golden Gate Park.

F-Market Streetcar Line Extension
San Francisco, CA, USA

Where chainlink fence once divided one of San
Francisco's main thoroughfares, the regal stature
of 25-foot (7.5-meter) tall Canary Island palms
brings prominence and pride to Upper Market
Street. Positive citywide response to the nostalgic
image of palms and vintage streetcars in this
residential section of Market Street has invited
independent national research on the effect of
public transportation projects on the larger
urban environment.

Portsmouth Square
San Francisco, CA, USA

The design of Portsmouth Square, the most
heavily used park in San Francisco's Chinatown,
expresses its central role in Chinatown as well as
its significance as San Francisco's first park.
Chinese culture is reflected in the buildings and
vegetation, while the park's historic importance
is alluded to by site furnishings and materials.

The park's upper level, completed in 1994, was
organized into three principal spaces: a family-
oriented area with a playground, rest rooms, and
small lawn; a central courtyard accommodating
large civic gatherings; and a forecourt to the
elevator serving the Portsmouth Square parking
garage below.

The Great Highway
Seawall/Promenade
San Francisco, CA, USA

The seawall/promenade was constructed along a .5-mile (.8 kilometer) section of the Great Highway as protection from winter storms, as well as to provide a 16-foot-wide (5-meter-wide) walkway for strollers. Stairways provide access to Ocean Beach below.

South Embarcadero Project
San Francisco, CA, USA

An area of a long-abandoned freight railway, dirt pathways, and warehouses has been renovated to become an innovative surface roadway corridor with a light-rail extension in the corridor center, both designed explicitly to create open space and ready access to the bay. A 25-foot-wide (7.5-meter-wide) bay-side pedestrian promenade and adjacent bike lane were installed to promote public enjoyment of bay views.

The entire boulevard is landscaped and includes London plane trees on the land-side sidewalk and more than five dozen Canary Island palm trees lining the medians on both sides of the railway. Streetscape elements reflect the waterfront of the past, with acorn-style light fixtures and custom-manufactured cobblestones.

Kezar Stadium
San Francisco, CA, USA

The 10.5-acre (4.2-hectare) stadium, a multipurpose athletic facility, was designed as an open, sensuous landform. Terraced stadium seating is balanced with broad expanses of lawn and uncut red fescue. Groves of large evergreen trees eventually will enclose the stadium, blending it into Golden Gate Park. Deciduous flowering species were used as accents along the promenade.

The ceremonial Kezar arch and the entry plaza are situated on the stadium's central longitudinal axis. The arch, which flanks the project's western edge, alludes to the architecture of the old stadium.

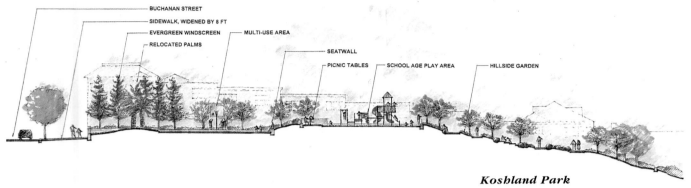

BUCHANAN STREET
SIDEWALK, WIDENED BY 8 FT
EVERGREEN WINDSCREEN — MULTI-USE AREA
RELOCATED PALMS
SEATWALL
PICNIC TABLES — SCHOOL AGE PLAY AREA
HILLSIDE GARDEN

Koshland Park
San Francisco, CA, USA

The proposed renovation of Koshland Park in the Hayes Valley is an example of the approach being taken by San Francisco to revitalize its neighborhood parks. The design concept emphasizes providing a variety of recreational areas: a large paved area for court games and social events, play areas for both tots and school-age children, a hillside landscape for passive recreation, and a community garden.

Environmental psychologists say that people have two fundamental needs regarding open public spaces: to have contact with others and with nature. The park's design is intended to satisfy these needs in a variety of settings, since the members of each age group have different ways of relating to one another and the landscape.

Alta Plaza Playground
San Francisco, CA, USA

Built playground elements composed of simple, recognizable shapes "float" within and/or above the sand, which is seen as a fluid material. Wood boardwalks connect these elements with the playground perimeter and provide informal seating.

The playground is intended to meet programmatic requirements while also inspiring both children and adults to dream. Structures were designed to be memorable and to possess poetic qualities sustaining children's interest long after they are familiar with the "play events" (slides, ladders, etc.).

Construction was inspired by Arts and Crafts architectural traditions, as seen in the wood structures, and classicism, evident in the cast-in-place octagonal concrete pavilion. Layout of decking heights and railing and roof detailing were custom designed to give the structures the character of playhouses on stilts. The railings also were intended to be more inviting to touch than the standard manufactured enclosure.

City and County of San Francisco
Landscape Architecture Section
Bureau of Engineering, Department
of Public Works
1680 Mission Street
San Francisco, CA 94103, USA
phone | 415-554-8285

Sasaki Associates, Inc.

Sasaki Associates combines creativity and problem solving to provide clients with comprehensive, integrated planning and design services. This approach grew out of founder Hideo Sasaki's belief that the most successful planning and design is accomplished by a team of experienced professionals from an array of design disciplines who work closely with the client to achieve the best solution.

Since the firm's founding in 1953, Sasaki Associates has addressed a range of projects that are diverse in scale and setting: clients from both the public and private sectors engage the firm's professional staff for waterfront and urban design assignments, corporate and commercial facilities design, college and institutional planning and design, roadway and transportation projects, large-scale land planning and community design, and specialty landscapes such as arboreta, gardens, parkways and atriums. A significant portion of Sasaki's practice is international in scope, especially in the area of tourism planning and development. The firm also has extensive expertise in public/private projects that involve a high degree of client and community input and the implementation of complex funding strategies.

An appreciation for context–which broadly encompasses physical setting, natural environment, history and culture, and the particular opportunities and constraints of the program–has consistently shaped and inspired Sasaki's work.

Newburyport Downtown and Waterfront
Newburyport, MA, USA

The design of Inn Street, once a derelict asphalt alley, incorporated traditional brick, reuse of existing granite curbs, granite cobblestones, bluestone stepping stones indicating access to adjacent buildings, new trees, and light fixtures modeled after an original fixture discovered in a turn-of-the-century photograph.

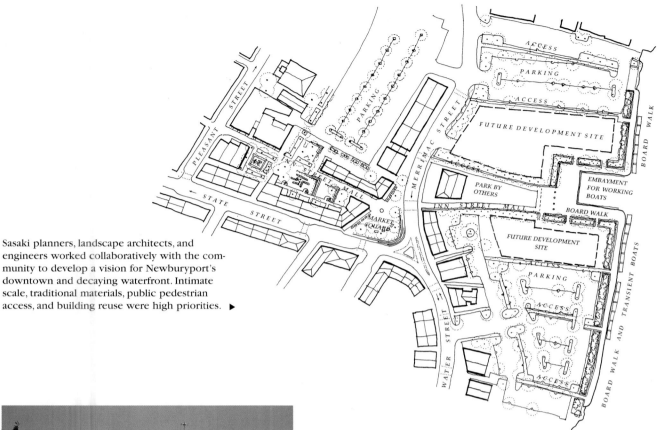

Sasaki planners, landscape architects, and engineers worked collaboratively with the community to develop a vision for Newburyport's downtown and decaying waterfront. Intimate scale, traditional materials, public pedestrian access, and building reuse were high priorities. ▶

▲
The historic embayment extends the boardwalk to provide access to working and pleasure boats, a year-round source of waterfront vitality. Heavy plantings of saltwater-tolerant trees and shrubs line the edge of the boardwalk to reduce the impact of winter winds.

▲
This playground, a place for children, parents, and senior citizens alike, was developed as an experiment at the west end of Inn Street. The owners of an existing shoe store and other newly restored shops and restaurants supported the idea of providing play and seating space to complement shopping activities.

Charleston Waterfront Park
Charleston, SC, USA

The 7-acre (2.8-hectare) park with its 1,300-foot-long
(390-meter-long) promenade has re-established the
link between the city's historic downtown and the
Cooper River. This view from an adja-cent building
encompasses the four-oak grove, great lawn, Pineapple Fountain and garden, and Palmetto Promenade
that connects Vendue Pier and Plaza to a soft
residential park and the restored Adgers Wharf.

▲
Symbolizing Charleston's commitment to hospitality,
the Pineapple Fountain is an abstract design in cast
stone and bronze leaf. The granite stepped detail at
the base and pool encourages public access to the
water and waterfalls.

Fountain Plaza
Buffalo, NY, USA

The 31,000 square-foot (2,790 square-meter) public plaza features a dramatic granite fountain and a skating rink that functions as a reflecting pool or lower level plaza in the summer. The Main Street light rail line defines the east edge of the space; to the south is an existing bank building; and to the west and north is a new mixed-use development that includes a public support building. The central plaza was built atop a parking garage, while the granite fountain and grove of trees were built at the existing grade.

Flagpoles with integrated lighting define the multipurpose plaza. Tall cluster lights illuminate the entire space, particularly during the winter months when the ice skating rink is in use. The water can be easily drained to allow the plaza to accommodate public activities such as art fairs, car shows, food festivals, and concerts.

Bent-iron benches surround pear trees in the fountain's grove setting. Illuminated glass blocks lie behind the two principal waterfalls in the summer, but when the fountain is turned off in winter the blocks become important as an abstract reference to water in sunlight.

Betty Marcus Park
Dallas, TX, USA

Located in the heart of the Dallas Arts District, which Sasaki also planned, the 0.75-acre (0.3-hectare) park was designed to complete the adjacent Myerson Symphony Center. A view from the Myerson Center roof illustrates the relationship of the green and pink granite-paved dining terrace, which is an extension of lobby dining, and the flowers, grove of trees, and water wall against busy Pearl Street.

The dining terrace is tucked into an intensely planted garden of groundcover and flowering shrubs. Cedar elm and red oak trees provide welcome shade and accommodate both up and down lights for nighttime enjoyment of this public park.
▼

▲
Public art is an important focus of the park,
providing additional experiences for visitors.
Performers are provided a lounge area that faces
and opens onto the west side of the park.

▲
Additional art, benches, and a water wall extend
the park from the performers' lounge to Flora
Street. The Cold Spring green granite weirs and
wall fountain disguise a very busy Pearl Street
some 15 feet (4.5 meters) below the park.
The entire park rests over a building, requiring
a highly creative solution to achieve required
planting depths and accommodate the additional
structural load.

Sasaki Associates, Inc.
64 Pleasant Street
Watertown, MA 02172, USA
phone | 617-926-3300
fax | 617-924-2748

900 N. Point Street
Suite B300
San Francisco, CA 94109, USA
phone | 415-776-7272
fax | 415-202-8970

The SWA Group

The SWA Group is a professional landscape design and planning practice offering capabilities for solving contemporary environmental and development problems. For more than three decades the firm has designed innovative and workable environments in a range of urban, suburban, and regional contexts throughout the United States and overseas. The SWA Group also has expertise in citizen involvement and processing of development permits, remote sensing and terrain analysis, and visual communications.

SWA has developed a national reputation in urban design. The firm's process carefully integrates design goals with infrastructure needs, providing policies and standards for creating and enhancing the visual quality of large-scale urban landscapes. In the area of land use planning, The SWA Group maintains expertise at both the urban and regional levels, emphasizing the creation of plans and policies that determine the amount, distribution, location, and phasing of uses and activities to achieve economic, social, and physical objectives.

The SWA Group maintains full-service offices in the San Francisco Bay Area and in Southern California; Houston and Dallas, Texas. The firm employs more than eighty-five professionals including landscape architects, urban designers, land planners, and specialists in imaging.

SWA's project experience includes urban renewal and design, planned communities, new towns, residential development, office complexes and corporate headquarters, industrial centers, research campuses, retail and mixed-use development, entertainment centers, parks and recreational facilities, golf communities and clubs, sports stadiums, resorts and hotels, civic and medical development, and schools and campuses.

Arizona Center
Phoenix, AZ, USA

Arizona Center is an eight-square-block mixed-use center set in a landscaped park. Here, a strongly patterned view from offices and hotel rooms shows a lower garden designed as an oasis with water and shade, bordered by tiered areas intricately planted with desert plants and flowers.

Designer: Bill Callaway

The gardens of Arizona Center draw in pedestrians and offer them shaded lanes, terraced views, rushing water, bright contrasts, natural fragrances, and softened light–surroundings not found elsewhere in downtown Phoenix.

Designer: Bill Callaway

▲
Dramatic canopies over walkways provide
shade during the day and intricate patterns
when lit at night.

More than nine hundred mature date palms
were planted for shade and to provide structure
to the design.
▼

Andover Companies Corporate Headquarters
Andover, MA, USA

The building and landscape reflect the client's desire for an image of stability, permanence, and timelessness–qualities appropriate for an insurance company.

Designer: Michael Sardina

Designer: Michael Sardina

▲ Mature trees preserved near the building give an immediate sense of the secure and timeless relationship of building to site.

Formal elements such as this tree-bordered path ▶ with its view of the building provide a symmetry in contrast with the forested surroundings.

Designer: Michael Sardina

Weyerhaeuser Corporate Headquarters
Tacoma, WA, USA

The large headquarters building is integrated into the forest by horizontal architecture that minimizes its size and creates the effect of a dam on one end of a man-made lake.

The refined quality of the architecture extends down the steps to clipped beds of ivy and a highly maintained lawn. The plantings provide a transition to the forest edge.

▲
At the east and west entrances, auto courts are defined by the rose-tinted, exposed aggregate patterns.

Designer: Jim Reeves

Williams Square
Las Colinas, TX, USA

At Williams Square, bronze sculptures of wild mustangs gallop across an open granite plaza and through an abstract running stream, reflecting the heritage of the Texas landscape.

At night, lighting provides a dramatic focus on the movement of the horses through the water.
▼

Designer: Jim Reeves

The bronze horses, created by sculptor Robert Glenn, are a counterpoint to the crisp geometry of the buildings and plaza.

Designer: Jim Reeves

Designer: Jim Reeves

▲
Fountains, placed to simulate splashes from the hooves of the running horses, add to the strong movement of the scene.

The SWA Group
2200 Bridgeway Boulevard
P.O. Box 5904, Sausalito, CA
94966-5904, USA
phone | 415-332-5100
fax | 415-332-0719

CLIENTS

Filnvest Development Corporation

Fujita Corporation

Hyatt Development Corporation

Intel Corporation

The Irvine Company

The Prime Group

The Rouse Company

Silicon Graphics

Skidmore, Owings & Merrill, LLP

Stanford University

Universal Studios

Walt Disney Imagineering

Don Vaughan Ltd.

The firm's projects range from the planning and design of major developments such as Whistler Village, the University of Victoria, and Concord Pacific Place to the design of urban plazas, parks, and a variety of multiple-family housing. Don Vaughan Ltd. focuses on the relationship of the landscape to water, incorporating native plant material when possible. In the 1970s and 1980s, the firm concentrated on redesigning urban Vancouver, British Columbia. Inspired by the still ponds and cascading waterfalls of the Millicoma River in Oregon, where he spent childhood summers, Don Vaughan brought this tranquil atmosphere to the urban plazas of Vancouver.

In addition to taking a leading role in several major projects, including the Whistler Village ski resort, and designing Discovery Square and the Dr. Sun Yat-Sen Garden in the mid-1980s, Vaughan put together a team of Vancouver's top landscape architects to produce the design and construction documentation for the site of the World's Fair on Vancouver's waterfront.

After Vaughan received a diploma in sculpture from the Emily Carr College of Art and Design in 1989, his work continued to incorporate water, but with a stronger sculptural component, as shown in such projects as Granite Assemblage at Ambleside Village in West Vancouver, the Howard Petch Fountain at the University of Victoria, and the fountain at Metrotown in Vancouver. Vaughan has also worked on the masterplan for Concord Pacific Place. This project included David Lam Park, with sculptures that encourage interaction with the intertidal zone and promote an awareness of Vancouver's 3-meter (10-foot) daily tidal difference.

Ambleside Park, Granite Assemblage
West Vancouver, British Columbia, Canada

In this waterfront park, Vaughan designed and sculpted a series of rough-split granite cubes, set and placed with apparent order at the water's edge, in an artificial tide pool extending into the park.

Metrotown Civic Plaza
Metrotown Shopping Centre
Burnaby, British Columbia, Canada

In the new shopping community of Metrotown in Burnaby, a civic plaza was incorporated with a fountain and granite sculpture as a focus.

University of Victoria
Victoria, British Columbia, Canada

Within the University of Victoria campus,
Vaughan designed a commemorative fountain
that has become a central focus point and a
gathering place for students throughout the year.

Whistler Village
Whistler, British Columbia, Canada

A resort village was planned and created at
the base of Whistler and Blackcomb Mountains.
The village serves as both a summer and winter
destination.

Designer: Eldon Beck/Don Vaughan

Dr. Sun Yat-Sen Garden
Vancouver, British Columbia, Canada

The 2.5-acre (1-hectare) classical Chinese Garden is part of the adjacent Chinese Cultural Center in Vancouver's Chinatown and was modeled after a Ming Dynasty Suzhou Merchant's Garden. Don Vaughan Ltd. and Joe Wai Architects worked in conjunction with Dr. Marwyn Samuels of the University of British Columbia and senior members of the Suzhou Garden as a team to design the garden.

Discovery Square
Vancouver, British Columbia, Canada

In the center of Vancouver's business district, Don Vaughan has been responsible for the design of the majority of the open spaces that relate both in form and materials to the city's architecture. The buildings become an integral part of the space providing shelter for park users and expanded open space for transit users.

Don Vaughan Ltd.
3069 Mathers Avenue
West Vancouver
British Columbia, V7V 2K3 Canada
phone | 604-922-1885
fax | 604-922-5485

Melville Street Plaza (Sun Life Plaza)
Vancouver, British Columbia, Canada

The fountain and plaza have been created as an oasis in the downtown core, creating a place for crowds or a single individual. The fountain is a stylization of the Millicoma River.

CLIENTS

Government of Canada, External Affairs

Canadian Museum of Civilization

Concord Pacific Developments Ltd.

Expo '86 Corporation

District of North Vancouver

Service Corporation (Canada) International

Sun Yat-Sen Garden Society

University of British Columbia

University of Victoria

Municipality of West Vancouver

Whistler Village Land Corporation

DIRECTORY

J. Robert Anderson, ASLA
Landscape Architect
1715 South Capitol of Tex. #105
Austin, TX 78746, USA
phone | 512-329-8882
fax | 512-329-8883

Andropogon Associates, Ltd.
374 Shurs Lane
Philadelphia, PA 19128, USA
phone | 215-487-0700
fax | 215-483-7520

Belt Collins Design Group
680 Ala Moana Boulevard, First Floor
Honolulu, HI 96813-5406, USA
phone | 808-521-5361
fax | 808-538-7819

A. E. Bye and Janis Hall
300 Central Park West
New York, NY 10024, USA
phone | 212-873-4615
fax | 212-873-4615

Dean Cardasis and Associates
32 Cosby Avenue
Amherst, MA 01002, USA
phone | 413-549-4937
fax | 413-548-8825

Carrick Design Inc.
255 Duncan Mill Road, Suite 302
Don Mills, Ontario M3B 3H9, Canada
phone | 416-447-6295
fax | 416-447-6334

Design Workshop, Inc.
1390 Lawrence Street, Suite 200
Denver, CO 80204, USA
phone | 303-623-5186
fax | 303-623-2260

Roger DeWeese Inc. and Associates (RDI&A)
13140 Carousel Lane
Del Mar, CA 92014, USA
phone | 619-794-9991
fax | 619-794-9998

du Toit Allsopp Hillier
50 Park Road
Toronto, Ontario M4W 2N5, Canada
phone | 416-968-9479
fax | 416-968-0687

EDSA
Edward D. Stone, Jr. & Associates, Inc.
1512 East Broward Boulevard, Suite #110
Fort Lauderdale, FL 33301, USA
phone | 954-524-3330
fax | 954-524-0177

Grissim/Metz Associates, Inc.
37801 Twelve Mile Road
Farmington Hills, MI 48331, USA
phone | 810-553-2500
fax | 810-553-2505

Grupo de Diseño Urbano
Fernando Montes de Oca no. 4
Colonia Condesa, México City
06140, México
phone | 52-5-553-1248
fax | 52-5-286-1013

Terence G. Harkness
Landscape Architecture/Planning
1023 West Charles Street
Champaign, IL 61821, USA
phone | 217-398-6308
fax | 217-244-4568

Hough Woodland Naylor Dance Limited
961 The East Mall, Suite B
Etobicoke, Ontario M9B 6K1, Canada
phone | 416-620-6577
fax | 416-620-9546

JMP Golf Design Group
14651 Big Basin Way
Saratoga, CA 95070, USA
phone | 408-867-5600
fax | 408-867-9680

Carol R. Johnson Associates Inc.
1100 Massachusetts Avenue
Cambridge, MA 02138, USA
phone | 617-868-6115
fax | 617-864-7890

Jones & Jones
105 South Main Street
Seattle, WA 98109, USA
phone | 206-624-5702
fax | 206-624-5923

John Tillman Lyle, FASLA
580 North Hermosa
Sierra Madre, CA 91024, USA
phone | 909-869-2684
fax | 909-869-4460

Steve Martino & Associates
3336 North 32nd Street, Suite 110
Phoenix, AZ 85018-6241, USA
phone | 602-957-6150
fax | 602-224-5288

Thomas McBroom Associates Ltd.
120 Carlton Street, Suite 305
Toronto, Ontario M5A 2K1, Canada
phone | 416-967-9329
fax | 416-967-7105

Moorhead Associates & Forrec Ltd.
211 Laird Drive
Toronto, Ontario M4G 3W8, Canada
phone | 416-696-8863
fax | 416-696-8866

Morgan Wheelock Inc.
362 Summer Street
Somerville, MA 02144, USA
phone | 617-776-9300
fax | 617-776-9333

Murase Associates, Inc.
1300 Northwest Northrup
Portland, OR 97209, USA
phone | 503-242-1477
fax | 503-295-0942

City of New York Parks & Recreation
Olmsted Center
Flushing Meadows-Corona Park
Flushing, NY 11368, USA
phone | 718-760-6613
fax | 718-760-6666

Cornelia Hahn Oberlander
1372 Acadia Road
Vancouver, British Columbia
V6T 1P6, Canada
phone | 604-224-3967
fax | 604-224-7347

Olin Partnership
421 Chestnut Street
Philadelphia, PA 19106, USA
phone | 215-440-0030
fax | 215-440-0041

ROMA Design Group
Architects and Planners
1527 Stockton Street
San Francisco, CA 94133, USA
phone | 415-616-9900
fax | 415-788-8728

City and County of San Francisco
Landscape Architecture Section
Bureau of Engineering
Department of Public Works
1680 Mission Street
San Francisco, CA 94103, USA
phone | 415-554-8285

Sasaki Associates, Inc.
64 Pleasant Street
Watertown, MA 02172, USA
phone | 617-926-3300
fax | 617-924-2748

The SWA Group
2200 Bridgeway Boulevard
P.O. Box 5904
Sausalito, CA 94966-5904, USA
phone | 415-332-5100
fax | 415-332-0719

Don Vaughan Ltd.
3069 Mathers Avenue
West Vancouver, British Columbia
V7V 2K3, Canada
phone | 604-922-1885
fax | 604-922-5485

PHOTO CREDITS

J. Robert Anderson, ASLA: p. 12, David Omer (top left, top right); p. 13, Elizabeth McGreevy (top right, bottom left); p. 14, Rick Patrick (bottom).

Andropogon Associates, Ltd.: p. 18, Lynn Crosby Gammill (top left), Edward Blake (top right); p. 19, Edward Blake (top); p. 22, Nicholas Kelsh (top).

Belt Collins Design Group: p. 24, Camera Hawaii, Inc. (bottom right); p. 25, Camera Hawaii, Inc. (top left); p. 26, Camera Hawaii, Inc. (top), Bill Schildge (bottom); p. 29, Michael French Photography (bottom).

A. E. Bye and Janis Hall: pp. 30–32, A. E. Bye (all); pp. 33–35, Janis Hall (all).

Carrick Design Inc.: pp. 42–43, Warren Marr (all); p. 44, Jeff Daniels; p. 45, Jeff Daniels (top); pp. 46–47, Warren Marr (all).

Design Workshop, Inc.: pp. 50–52, Karen Keeney (all).

du Toit Allsopp Hillier: p. 60, Ewald Richter (bottom left, bottom right); p. 61, Steven Evans (top), Curt Clayton and University of Windsor (bottom); p. 62, Robert Burley/Design Archive (top), John Hillier (bottom).

Grissim/Metz Associates, Inc.: p. 72, Balthazar Korab Ltd. (bottom); p. 73, Balthazar Korab Ltd. (top, bottom); pp. 74–75, Balthazar Korab Ltd. (all); p. 76, Korab Hedrich Blessing, Inc. (all); p. 77, Balthazar Korab Ltd.

Grupo de Diseño Urbano: p. 82, Michael Calderwood (bottom left), Gabriel Figueroa F. (bottom right); pp. 83–84, Gabriel Figueroa F. (all); p. 85, Michael Calderwood (top), Gabriel Figueroa F. (bottom); p. 86, Gabriel Figueroa F. (all); p. 87, Michael Calderwood (top), Gabriel Figueroa F. (bottom).

Hough Woodland Naylor Dance Limited: p. 94, Adrian Oosterman; p. 95, Christopher Dew (bottom left); p. 96, Ian Dance (top), Nelson French (middle right, bottom left); p. 99, Steven Evans.

JMP Golf Design Group: p. 100, Brian Morgan; p. 102, Joann Dost (all); p. 103, Mike Klemme (top).

Carol R. Johnson Associates Inc.: p. 106, Jerry Howard; p. 107, Jerry Howard (all); p. 108, John Gustavsen (bottom); p. 109–110, Jerry Howard (all); p. 111, Alex S. Maclean.

Jones & Jones: p. 112, Michael Parker (all); p. 114, Michael Parker (top left); p. 115, Roger Turk, Northlight Photography (top), Randy Shelton Photography (bottom); p. 116, Randy Shelton Photography (all).

Steve Martino & Associates: p. 125, Richard Maack.

Thomas McBroom Associates Ltd.: p. 130, Michael French; pp. 131–134, Wayne Barrett, Barrett & MacKay Photography (all); p. 135, Peter Sellar.

Moorhead Associates & Forrec Ltd.: p. 137, Lawrence Raskin (all); p. 138, HOCO Ltd. (bottom left); p. 139, Ian Clifford (top); p. 141, Forrec Design Europe (bottom).

Morgan Wheelock Inc.: p. 142, Steve Rosenthal (top left); pp. 144–145, Ann Fuller (all); p. 146, Ann Fuller (top), Thomas Shelby (bottom).

Landscape Architecture: The Heart of the Matter (essay): p. 149, photo courtesy of James Rose Center.

Murase Associates, Inc.: p. 152, Timothy Hursley; p. 153, Bruce Forster (top right, bottom center); p. 157, Timothy Hursley (top and bottom).

City of New York Parks & Recreation: p. 159, James Mituzas (all); p. 160, James Mituzas (top left); p. 162, James Mituzas (all).

Cornelia Hahn Oberlander: p. 164, Milton Hicks (top), Elisabeth Whitelaw (bottom); p. 165, Kiku Hawkes; p. 166, Elisabeth Whitelaw (top, middle); p. 168, Elisabeth Whitelaw (all); p. 169, Elisabeth Whitelaw (all).

Olin Partnership: p. 170, Alistair McIntosh (top).

ROMA Design Group: p. 176, Jane Lidz (left), Aerial Images (right); p. 178, Jane Lidz (top left), Aerial Images (bottom); p. 179, Aerial Images; p.181, Aerial Images.

Sasaki Associates, Inc.: All photographs by Sasaki Associates.

The SWA Group: p. 194, Dixi Carrillo (left), Tom Fox (right); p. 195, Dixi Carrillo (top, bottom); p. 196, Tom Fox (all); p. 197, Dixi Carrillo (top), Gerry Campbell (bottom left, bottom right); pp. 198–199 Tom Fox (all).

Don Vaughn Ltd.: p. 201, Anthony Redpath (left, top right); p. 202, Anthony Redpath (top).